VINTAGE
CLOTHING
1880-1960
Identification & Value Guide

by Maryanne Dolan

ISBN 0-89689-039-2

BOOKS AMERICANA
INC

COVER

Antique Lace Dress
LAVENDER & LACE
Haute Couture

Model
SANDRA LOGAN

for my mother,

A 'FASHION PLATE'

ACKNOWLEDGEMENTS:

ACKNOWLEDGEMENTS:

With much gratitude to those who loaned their treasures:
Maryls Aboudara
Nan Almeida
Paige Baca
Linda Baker
Virginia Cox
Beatrice Deasy
Margaret Fitch
Clarice Hart
Betty Krueger
Pearline Munson
and to those who modeled:
Jennifer Alley
Betty Luther
Ruth Richter
Sue Rasmussen
Ann Thatcher
Pam Thatcher
Lynda Weir
Special thanks to:
Oona of Oona's Vintage Fashions, Oakland California
Alison Paula Jaret, American Home Sewing Assn, NY
Jenny Oparski of Butterick Fashion Marketing Co., NY
Elise Amour of FOLKWEAR PATTERNS, San Rafael, CA
The Southern Oregon Historical Society of Jackson, OR
and the many dealers and collectors throughout the country
who have shared their knowledge and talents.

TABLE OF CONTENTS

INTRODUCTION

Collecting vintage fashion becomes the art of the possible. The very material of which most clothing was made lends itself to destruction and the need to be in fashion which caused so many beautiful gowns to be discarded and neglected has left us with many gaps in our collection wardrobes.

Even the Smithsonian Institution has not been able to fully round out the Inaugural Gown collection of the First Ladies. Some of the gowns currently on exhibit were never worn to that First Ball, but are simply dresses of the period. So it is with the collector; if a primary sample of a period piece is not available, we must make do with a secondary example, or a dress or suit of the same period.

Indeed, so much High Fashion has been chronicled that a whole new wave of collectors dealing only with every day garments has surfaced, but most collectors today, are seeking good samples of the great design periods, and this is a challenging, but rewarding task.

It can take you from specialized shops, to flea markets, to thrift shops, to second hand clothing stores and to friends and relatives with bulging closets or attics.

Competition in this field is becoming much keener and it behooves you to be pleasant to Aunt Minnie who may be harboring a Balenciaga somewhere.

Fortunately for us, many people refuse to discard anything and it is to them that we owe a large debt of gratitude for much of our older clothing. In most cases, since these people bothered to save it, they also took care of it.

Unless you are blessed with great skill at needlework, older clothing is often difficult to repair and restore with authenticity. The old taffeta, for example, had metallic thread to give it that rustle, but it also caused it to rot away, so you seldom see an old taffeta dress in mint condition and it is almost impossible to repair. The best advice is to take your restorable, valuable clothing to an expert. In many cases museums dealing with vintage clothing offer such services, and if they do not, can probably recommend a specialist in this narrow field.

If the price is right, and the damage slight or not too obvious, buy the piece and then think about restoration. "If the Price is Right" should be emblazoned above every clothing collector's closet these days when the large auction houses are organizing special auctions of high vintage fashion clothing and selling it for high sums.

The average collector today should keep in mind the fragility of his or her collectible, the competition for this clothing, the escalating prices and need for less procrastination. Someone, if it's a fair price, will buy that gorgeous gown before you can say Schiaparelli.

Collectors should look for rare pieces in good condition, the choice Victorian pieces or the 20's dresses that are beaded and in excellent

1881 fashion scene. Courtesy of Butterick Archives.

condition. Remember that all of the 1920's dresses were not hand beaded but that does not seem to be of tremendous import to collectors; what should rank very high on your list of requirements for any garment is the basic design, the material, and the way the garment was made.

The vintage clothing collector has chosen a field which excels in great beauty and interest; it deals with design, with fabrics of types sometimes rare and expensive, with braids and lace, and feathers and beads; it makes a definitive comment on history and what people did and what they wore for their work and leisure. It is often a collectible of remarkable elegance and above all it is a reflection on the collector, for anyone who chooses this field must be a person of awareness and taste.

The collection should speak for itself, through you, and the statement it makes says as much about you, the collector, as it does about the person who originally wore it.

AUTHOR'S NOTE: As the first book in the area of pricing vintage clothing there will no doubt be omissions or differences of opinion. I should welcome your comments and suggestions in keeping this guide current.

CHAPTER ONE
1880 - 1900

The primary collecting area in the field of Vintage Fashion occurs after 1880, beyond that we are dealing with the very rare and expensive garment which has now become the province of the museums and affluent collector. True, the occasional 1860's or 1870's dress or hat or bonnet will turn up to lend excitement to the chase, but the practical collector will choose a later period which lends itself to easier acquisitions.

By the 1880's the bustle using a wire support was back in style and the feet were visible below a slightly shortened skirt. That seemed to be as far as women were allowed to display any part of the anatomy, and unfortunately for females of the 1880's and 1890's, fashion dictated such a plethora of clothing for ordinary wear that one wag was inspired to say that planning the Parthenon probably took less time than his wife's daily toilette.

Too true, imagine yourself day after dreary day preparing to go outdoors; the corset, the drawers, the bodice, petticoats and more petticoats, and often so many buttons down the back help was needed to dress.

The Victorians loved clutter in all things, their houses were shrines to that particular god, knick-knacks everywhere, not an inch of shelf or table space left unoccupied. It seems fitting then that the women who dictated these arrangements also cluttered their persons. Not only was the clothing complicated and overdone, but the coiffure was also a tribute to the complex, calling for front curls and whatever one favored in back. False hairpieces were popular, some made from the combings of the Victorian woman herself; braids, or plaits as they were referred to, chignons, loops; the more elaborate the better.

Ribbons and feathers and flowers were much in evidence on the bonnets which were so varied and eyecatching they are greatly prized today by collectors.

The 1880's bustle differed from that of the 1870's, but the whole effect in the first years of the 1880's was one of rigidity and stiffness, which ironically or not, complemented the Victorian attitudes.

Dresses were heavier, and skirts began to increase in size.

Men's clothing was somber and conformed to the new image of the successful industrialist. Single-breasted jackets and straightline, longish, frock coats, worn with straight trousers without a crease, prevailed. The clothing atmosphere was one of inflexibility and propriety, and in female fashion, not always particularly pretty.

From her well-shod feet to her beribboned bonnet, the lady of the 1880's was as encased by her clothing as she was by the conventions of the day. For the collector of the fashions of those years, the clothes are highly desirable, but not readily available. It is wise to comb attics and old trunks, especially if your family has been an acquisitive one, for it is usually in this way that the collector has the best chance of coming upon these treasures.

To us, in 1983, they seem as other-worldly as the 17th century laces and satins must have seemed to the Victorian, they were uncomfortable, restrictive and not overly flattering, but they appeal to our fantasy lives, says one dealer, and the best of the clothing represents good workmanship and often good design in what was an era of peace and plenty and sturdy family life. The garments are part of that nostalgia, they have an aura of stability.

One of the loveliest of all collectibles springs from the 1880's — the shawl. Shawls are still worn today, they are useful and graceful, but the biggest thing in shawls for the Victorian lady was Paisley. The colorful, swirled patterns of abstract, curved shapes are felt to have derived from the patterns of Persian rugs and the name itself from Paisley, Scotland. It was far and away the most popular type, although these shoulder coverings came in a great variety of sizes and materials. If the budget does not lend itself to the dresses and suits of the Victorian age, try shawls, with their heavy fringes and bright colors they can be used in a variety of ways, even as wall hangings. They are still fairly easy to find although serious collectors have long been seeking them and there are now many museum displays which feature them. They are without doubt, one of the genuine markers of the age and some collectors use them as a backdrop to a clothing collection.

As the 1880's gave way to the 1890's the silhouette began to show signs of adapting to the emerging woman. Paris still had a firm hold on the fashion world, although women were showing signs of making their own decisions about what they wanted to wear and how they wanted to look. Men too, began to feel stifled, but in spite of the tendencies of a group called the 'Aesthes' with their fancy vests and velvet jackets and their preference for color, the basic shape did not change much. The accessories were engaging though, and lent an air of the rakish to the men of fashion — the cane, the elegant watches, the fobs, the hats — all of which are diligently hunted today.

By the 1890's the shape of the female gown had become softer and looser. The sleeve, always a good indicator of the period of early clothing, now showed some fullness at the top and by the late 1890's had expanded considerably.

But the biggest revolution in clothing was caused by the wheel. Or two wheels — the bicycle. It became an absolute passion and while we may find it hard to conceive of cycling with large, veiled hats and full length skirts and often rather formal looking blouses, think of the men doomed to hats and coats and ties while they pedaled. Still, after being repressed for so long the bicycle must have seemed like the ultimate in freedom. Where the wealthy had their horses and carriages, now everyone could indulge the craving for mobility at little expense. Naturally, not everybody was content to ride as if dressed for a party, so it was only natural that clothing modification would follow.

The bustle disappeared. Knickebockers became the number one item on the fashion agenda. Both men and women wore them and the difference was the women's were much fuller. Hats were still worn, and jackets but men adopted the cap too, and younger boys really admired this casual style. The whole 1890's world was cycling, everybody was on the move. Skirts eventually replaced the knickers for women and they were full and easy to manage. Women's Lib wasn't even a gleam in the female eye, but the clothes were telling us something.

The 1890's female preferred such materials as gauze, and the old time silk warp challies, black taffeta was still popular and cashmeres and organdies and a new canvas cloth in fancy weave called 'Mouline natte' flourished. Transparent fabrics such as grenadine, mousseline de soie, chiffon and the small standing collar became part of the fashion scene, especially for Spring. Flowers, vines, scrolls, trimmings of blossoms and leaves covering these light fabrics lent a feminine look.

"Eighteen ninety eight," boasted a woman's magazine, "was a time to buy stripes, and all cord effects are safe for the coming season. Tucks will run crosswise on waist and sleeves and around the skirt, while braids, insertions, ruffles and all decoration will follow in the same path." Ruffles did indeed flourish in every possible width on that year's Summer fashions to such an extent that they often overshadowed the gown itself. Collectors today who find a gown of that era in less than repairable condition, tend to strip it of its laces and ruffles for possible use elsewhere. Do not overlook the possibilities of a gown in very poor condition which may cost too much to have refurbished. If the price is right, its trimmings, even to the buttons, can be useful as a collectible.

The seven gore skirt was in vogue and if you have the good fortune to own or to be able to examine a skirt made in this way, it is clearly a clever way of fitting the garment smoothly across the front and hips and giving it a graceful fullness at the back. For those interested, not only in the clothing of that day, but the way it was made, this type skirt has a dip in the back which is given more by the bias back seam than by the added length at the bottom. In certain materials, such as wool, this was a rather flowing cut and flattering. Wool, was a favorite for clothing of this period and much of it is still in surprisingly good condition.

The late 1800's allowed for almost any color, any material or shape in women's dresses, although black dominated colorwise and the foulard again was gaining favor. Although the name 'foulard' is used again and again in fashion writings of the day and we can assume that it communicated itself immediately to the women who read the writings, it is not something most of us hear much about today. It encompasses several fabrics, it is a lightweight twill or plain woven silk, or silk and cotton, and it usually has a small printed design. The fabrics used in the more expensive gowns of the late 1800's were made over using the original material. Sometimes this was done more than once so if the needlewoman was skilled, we often cannot date a dress accurately.

White crepe de chine sounds seductive now, and indeed it was meant to be then. Dresses made of this often have fascinating trim, narrow lace ruffles, or deep ruffles edged with lace. This silk crepe makes any garment we find today expensive, but it is usually quite beautiful.

Sleeves of that day were distinctive and more than anything else give the garments the look we most associate with the period. They were generally long and trimmed at the top, cuffs or edgings were usually seen at the wrist. By the turn of the century, the ideal, unrealistic goal in waistlines was 19 inches. They were cases of ruined health by women seeking the impossible.

The designers were handling fashion as if it were great art. The upper sleeves were very large and full and balanced horizontally with the hem of the skirt, but the eye was drawn inevitably to the tiny waist. It is an exercise in proportion and these designers did their work so well that it is the silhouette which comes to mind, rather than individual garments when we think of the late 1890's.

It would probably send the Victorian lady into a state of shock if she realized that collectors of 1983 are madly seeking her underwear. Back to Basics might well designate collections of undergarments of the 1880-1890 period. There is more underclothing available to the collector than would seem possible, probably because women wore so much of it, a goodly quantity of it has survived. The underthings were cleverly engineered to nip in or add on, tighten or disguise. Nobody's perfect, so there was plenty of it made, and plenty of it now to choose from.

The corset is legendary and one wonders today how women were ever coerced into wearing them. They were linen covered, shaped with whalebone or steel. The whalebone lent flexibility to the corset and was not so heavy as the steel, but in either case the corset could be considered a dangerous garment. Smelling salts were big sellers and it probably had to do with the tight corset.

Today we look on these as high collectibles, particularly from a museum standpoint. Several major museums have mounted showings of the corset, and in this kind of viewing they do have a certain fascination, and in the abstract, were often beautifully made, from a practical standpoint women of the 1980's should give daily thanks for their liberation from this undergarment.

It's questionable who suffered more from this fashion — the Right Whale which almost became extinct or the woman who wore the corset. It is not rare to find these, especially those with the steel ribs. Some have been found in the original boxes in pristine condition. Even then there were women who refused to conform or was it just faint heart?

Drawers, which are simply a takeoff of longish underpants are a wonderful addition to a collection. They are charming in an innocent, long-ago sense. They were meant to cover the 'limbs' and were popular for a very long time. Most of the surviving drawers, and indeed a surprising number have survived, are elegantly ribboned and trimmed with lace, but even the simpler ones are real conversation pieces. These undergarments, unless unusually elaborate, are more easily cared for than the dresses or suits since their basic material was cotton or muslin. It is a fast growing segment of the vintage clothing field.

Another interesting and overlooked collectible is the apron.

For everyday household chores, the apron was in full swing in the 1880-1890 period. The lifestyle of women still dictated their almost total commitment to the home and although women were beginning to emerge into the workforce, house and hearth was still the lodestar of their existence. So aprons were not only necessary, but fashion magazines of the day spent much space discussing their covering. Nowadays the apron is an anachronism except the frothy little concoctions we tend to don during the holiday season, or the barbecue aprons sported by men who feel more in the cordon bleu spirit when the voluminous garment is covering them.

The 1890's lifestyle dictated the use of the apron.

Afternoon tea was an ordinary aspect of life and demanded a covering for the dress of the young lady who did the pouring. These were fancy, net or lace, made in any way the owner chose, but reaching to the knee and made rather narrow. Some exist of Valenciennes or Brussels lace with very elaborate trimmings. There were fancywork aprons for needlework — embroidery was popular because even at leisure hands should not be idle — and, of course, the ordinary work-a-day aprons. These were generally about two-thirds length and were made of lawn, nainsook or dimity, but were also trimmed to relieve the plainness. These materials could be laundered fairly easily, a necessity for the working apron.

The apron wardrobe was large and diverse. There were sewing aprons, servants aprons, nurses aprons, the aprons artists wore, kitchen aprons, children's aprons and most interesting of all as a social commentary, the aprons worn by the new young women who were beginning to take jobs. They worked behind the counters or were moving into offices as 'typewriters'. To cover their clothing they wore simple aprons of black cambric or sateen which was made of 2 lengths of material hemmed together to a belt and either buttoned in back or tied with long, black strings. These reached the bottom of the skirt and had at least one pocket. These intrepid women also wore cuffs which often matched the apron.

Very few vintage clothing collectors have, as yet, focused on this area, but it is interesting and often delightful. It is challenging too, but a good, representative collection of aprons could be made from the 1880's to the 1980's, and it is as yet an inexpensive way to collect.

Aprons are beginning to appear in the shops, many reminiscent of a very different lifestyle. Not so glamorous as the designer clothing, or even the less costly pretty day dresses, aprons are a relatively untapped field, different, and because they are available and reasonably priced, rewarding.

These lesser collectibles within the large category of Vintage Fashion can be formed into deep and valuable categories of objects, certain to appreciate in value as well as interest, so always keep the accessories in mind when you buy older clothing.

Accessories were abundant in pre-1900 America. There was such a myriad of things with which to complement an ensemble that the mind boggles. Fashion maintained that these little trifles could be added to suit one's individual taste, and so the belts were often jeweled with precious gems or imitation stones, but silver and turquoise were favorites for the shirtwaist costume, emeralds and gold for blouses of velvet. Gold filigree belts were in vogue and the waist fell to the hemline and all manner of clever sash arrangements, as well as chiffon or lace or silk neck arrangements which tied under the chin were worn. Such short tie arrangements are still seen.

Veils were considered in fashion although ladies were warned that if the veils were dotted and "if the dots are too close, they will throw shadows on the face, but if scattered widely will have a flattering effect." Another typical fashion which seems forever etched in our consciousness is the empire scarf which was over 2 yards long and was meant to be fastened about the brim of the hat, crossed at the back and brought around and knotted on the left shoulder. A very romantic picture this, but not many seem to have survived. A favorite for this kind of scarf was Palin Brussels net so we are sometimes deceived into looking for chiffon and gauze and bypass the net.

Somewhat larger fans, feather ones or net or silk or gauze; suede gloves and suede dancing slippers were all the crack, and are all to be ardently embraced when discovered, fan collectors have long been active, but gloves are still, for the most part, lying in piles in out of the way boxes in shops, and they are still in the bargain category.

The freedoms which were coming were certainly manifesting themselves in fashion. Whereas black stockings had been de rigueur, now plaids or stripes, even embroidered effects replaced the rather elegant black, and polka dot hosiery was said to be a big seller. For the collector, finding a pair of hose of this era is a tremendous find. Usually when they are available, it is hosiery which had never been worn and simply laid away. Just as today the stockings were not much considered, and having served their purpose were discarded. Probably it is best to consider the hosiery a bonus to your clothing collection, never stop looking for it, but don't expect to find it too often. Recently I saw a pair of Victorian spats for $30. Condition was excellent and before I could say, "I'll take them, they were bought by someone more decisive than I. Anything to do with the years 1880-1890 will sell because it can no longer be treated lightly, it is definitely museum bait.

Combs too, have always had their devotees. The comb suited the pompadour hair style very well and were ornate and bejeweled and bedazzled the onlooker with multi-colored stones. There are many quite large and lovely comb collections already in existence, and not every clothing collector includes examples, although a comb lends authenticity to the dress. In collecting garments it is well to remember their context and if possible, to add a few of the accessories typical of their period. Even the august Smithsonian Institution has begun to equate the First Ladies gown collection with the rooms and artifacts of their times. If a collector strives to add some good quality items which tend to be silent pointers to the era, it can only add interest and piquancy.

Children's fashions have always had appeal. Probably during the 1880-1890 period, it was Kate Greenaway who most influenced their design. This popular artist of the 1890's depicted children dressed much as they would have been a century earlier, in the 1880's the Little Lord Fauntleroy look was introduced by the illustrations in the novel, the black velvet suit with a lace collar and plumed hat. A television rerun of the old film recently held a group of young people in thrall, so who knows what the future holds for little boys clothes.

Children seem always to have had more freedom in their clothing than the adults of the same time, and of course the infants were dressed in long dresses regardless of their sex. One of the great guides in this field are the old catalogues if precise dating is desired, but in the case of children, clothes were often handed down and may have been worn years after their purchase. From about the end of World War I, the whole world wanted to look young, and both children and adults wore much the same styles. Children's clothing is rather specialized, it tends to be expensive when the garment is old and attractive, and not all dealers handle it. It certainly lends authenticity to a collection and should be actively sought out if your aim is for all clothing of a certain period. People who love this type of apparel could not choose a more endearing type, if you do buy the dresses and suits worn by youngsters, search assiduously for the shoes, they are very special.

As in any collecting field, the fashion collector should be aware of developing trends. Today the Victorian wedding gown is one of the most desired of all garments. Young women are buying them to use just as they were originally intended and this fits into the general passion we all have for nostalgia.

Actually, the white gown and veil with orange blossoms was a Victorian invention. The gown was not meant to be put away after the wedding, it was to be used as a formal dress, or evening dress. My great grandmother's wedding dress of the 1880's shows much wear indicating it did double duty long after the wedding itself, it was not put away after the ceremony in tissue and into the cedar chest. It had never been intended for that fate.

The Victorian wedding dress can be magnificent, the best of them are overwhelming. The long train, the sleeves, full at the top, the luxurious fabric and the veil, often of precious lace crowned with either artificial or real orange blossoms. Not all of them had the large sleeves or the train and some are very simple, which proves once again that accurate dating in clothing is sometimes difficult.

While details have significance for the collector, it is more important to try to date by period divisions as suggested in this guide, otherwise, overlapping motifs which appeared and reappeared, and the fact that not everyone was prosperous enough to keep up with minor stylistic influences makes the average collector's task a considerable one. Even museums, unless given exact dates by the donor, generally use at least a decade time span.

Underwear is a good example of difficulty in precise dating.

Much of it was handmade following broad fashion dictates and while seeming to conform to a specific time, can often stem from an entirely different time, so it is best to use the famous 'circa' instead of dealing in specific years.

As 1900 dawned the most memorable thing about the late 1800's left its imprint. It was the shape of the female form. As sleeves continued to grow larger at the top and the skirt narrowed over the hips, the emphasis shifted to the tiny waist. Mention the gay nineties to anyone, the vision it conjures up is invariably that flamboyant, wasp waisted charmer.

Woman's trouseau set. Three pieces, nightwear. Peignoir, nightgown and drawers, lace and cotton, silk ribbon initialed 'B', c. 1890. Value, set $300-325.

Elaborate nightdress, c. 1880. Muslin with crochet trim. Value $145-165.

Gentleman's shirt, c. 1879-1880. Value $50-60.

White cambric nightgown, crocheted straps and bodice, tucked and ruffled nightcap. C. 1885. Nightgown, value $100-150. Nightcap, vlaue $30-45.

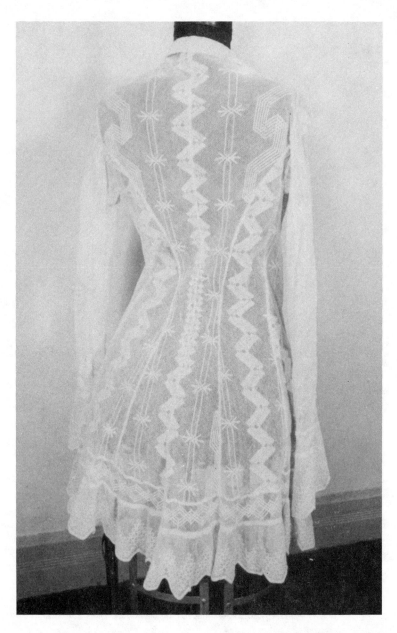

Late victorian white crocheted house jacket, princess type seams create a beautifully fitted garment. This is photographed on a 1909 patented dress form by Hallborchert Dress Form Co., NY, Chicago. Value of jacket $170-200.

Gentleman's nightshirt, cotton, button front, small pearl buttons, crocheted edging at front and sleeves, c. 1880. Value $65-85.

Worth of Paris gown, tussah silk, with train, c. 1898, known to have been worn in 1900. Value $2,000-2,500.

Victorian blouse with silk corde applique which is different from most blouses of the time. Probably worn with a full skirt with bustle in back. Notice how blouse is cut in back to accomodate the bustle. Tied at waist to form pigeon breasted look. All hand made. Value $350-400.

See-through lace over rust colored taffeta underdress. Known to have been worn about 1890. Value $250-285.

Figured silk apricot colored gown, 1890. Value $325-350. Photo by Kenn Knackstedt. Courtesy Southern Oregon Historical Society.

Victorian combing jacket, machine made lace, silk satin ribbon insets, lined with blue silk. Value $300-350.

Dark green and amber silk short jacket, high banded neckline of lace over silk, lace bodice. C. 1880-1885. Value $325-345.

1883 Black Mourning dress, gathers in front, ornamented back, trimmed with black jet beads. Value $375-425.

1880 dress. Black and white, characteristic of the second Victorian bustle period. Black velvet fitted bustle jacket, lace dress trimmed with velvet. Black ebony handled parasol trimmed with Spanish lace. Wool hat with cock feathers. Dress, value $550-600 (with jacket). Hat, $100-125.

Late 1870's style dress. Made of light blue wool, trimmed with brown velvet. It is accented by a high collared silk blouse. Undergarments consist of a corset and wired bustle. This dress, as shown, is a 1979 copy of an authentic dress in the collection of the State Historical Society of Wisconsin and patterns may be obtained from them. The original pattern has been altered to add the collar, wide cuffs and an extra ruffle to the skirt. Hat is of brown velvet with tinted feathers. Hatbox from Dobbs, Fifth Avenue, NY. Purse is of brown velvet to match the dress. Costume appraised at $500. Approximate cost of materials, $170.

1884 Wedding dress. Satin and lace. Lace fischu at neck. Value $500-600. Parasol, $145-165. Photo courtesy of Southern Oregon Museum, Kenn Knackstedt, photographer.

2 piece suits, 1898, including a lightweight bicycling outfit. Top, 2 pieces, value $300-350. Center, 2 pieces, $300-350. Bottom, 2 pieces, shorter skirt, $350-375.

Visiting costume, 1891. Fur trimmed. Value $700-750.

Garden party costume, 1891. "It seems," says the magazine fashion editor, "that everybody has gone mad about neck ruffles and stocks. Value $650-700.

1894. French dinner gown. Huge leg-o-mutton sleeves which fit so closely at the lower part of the arm that buttons and button holes are necessary "so that when the sleeve is on the fullness may be rumpled up like a glove and draped to suit the wearer's caprice." Value $650-700.

An autumn fete costume, 1894. Cocoa brown with very large leg-o-mutton sleeves. Velvet, striped ribbon trim. Value $600-700.

Front and back views of 1882 trade card of Bronner & Co.'s catalogue of Fashions for Spring and Summer. Clothing of this type is almost unobtainable but price ranges for the garments worn by the younger children in the cart are $35-50 for the hats, boys suit $85-100, girl's dress, $100-125. Older children's outfits, girl's long jacketed suit, Value $150-175. Boy's two piece suit, $150-175. High shoes worn by both. Each pair, $55-75. Straw hats, each $50-65.

BUTTERICK'S PATTERNS FOR BOYS.

Boy's fashions, 1867. Courtesy of Butterick Archives.

C. 1897-98 straw hat with plumes, $135-150. Wool poplin suit, $400-425. Notice jeweled belt, often these were genuine stones. Kid gloves, French, $28-38.

Straw hat, with long taffeta ribbons, floral, ribbon and net trim, c. 1890. Value $65-85.

Hat, straw with satin trim, c. 1898. Value $60-80.

1894 advertisement. Coats and cloaks of this type are now in the $350-400 range without fur; with fur trim depending on the kind, the price rises at least to the $500-600 range.

New York fashions of 1871. Courtesy of Butterick Archives.

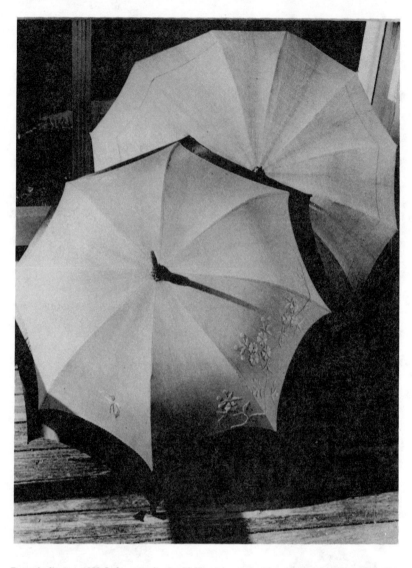

Parasols, linen, c. 1880. Left, cream linen with blue trim, embroidery. Folding wood handle, still in original box. Value $145-165. Right, tan linen, plain, long wooden handle. Value $95-120.

CHAPTER TWO
1900-1920

The Edwardian era was a long one. It began at the turn of the century and continued until 1910. So the collector can appreciate that although there were modifications of dress and accessories during these years, the tendency is to label all clothing of the period "Edwardian". It has a lovely ring to it and much of the clothing was as elegant and attractive as the classification.

Paris was still the center of fashion and at this fountainhead the wealthy still worshipped.

Actually the clothes of the Edwardian years did not differ significantly from those of the preceding Victorian era.

Frock coats were still correct formal day wear for men, the female waists were still as small as could be managed, and the 'S bend' shape was achieved by tightly laced corsets. There was fullness at the front of the bodice and the skirt was long and bell-shaped. This is one time when emphasis was not on youth, many of the fashion photos and paintings show a mature, full-blown woman.

Although the designation "Edwardian" derived from the years of rule of King Edward of England, the term has become one which encompasses the age of that particular style. The years before 'the war to end all wars' were opulent ones for those who could afford it. The characteristics of the clothing took on the characteristics of the lifestyle; the very large, highly ornamented hats, the high built up hairdo, the standing collar on gowns, feathers, laces and anything else which was thought to enchance the female figure.

Some of the accessories to men's wear, the separate collars in their charming boxes, cuff links and their boxes, collar buttons and their receptacle, all make delightful collectibles.

The whole of fashion was dictated by the way people lived and while lifestyles may alter, fabrics may gain and lose favor, hemlines may go up or down, human habits die hard.

In the early years of the new century, a woman's magazine was noting the carelessness of some women's dress, and complaining about "those careless Cinderellas who go about in curl papers, flappy old wrappers and decrepit shoes through half the day and blossom out in belated splendor toward evening." Today there are those who decry hair rollers in the supermarket and the eternal, uniform tight jeans. Indeed the amusing list of worst-dressed women circulated each year is simply a commentary on one man's opinion of the way celebrities fail the accepted norms of dress. It is always difficult to argue with personal taste and preference is everyone's right, but 'Good Taste Costs No More' as Mr. Gump said and it is interesting that even in today's permissive society you hear echoes of notions of taste which prevailed in the 1900's.

This was a time when the house gown or wrapper became a major part of the average woman's daily life, and very often these were the product of home sewing, or were homemade as the more affluent were wont to label them. These wrappers were so widely used because they were a respite from the torturous corsets, and were loose and comfortable. The less expensive ones were made of calico, percale or flannelette and were made in the same way as the gowns, standing or small collar, cape effects over the sleeves and usually flounced at the bottom of the skirt. These inexpensive items sold for less than a dollar, and now if they can be found they cost $125 and up.

Nineteen hundred was a fairly enlightened fashion time in that it recognized the reality of women's figures, notably that "stout women" were a large segment of the buying public and needed flattering garments. They were frankly referred to in literature of the day as 'plump' and 'stout'. Nowadays there is a distinct trend to satisfying the "large woman" or man. This is a departure for general fashion, some advertisements are featuring size 38 or 40 models, not merely in the abstract to suggest the full figure, but with photographs. Sighs of appreciation can be heard not only from women themselves but from some men who have always found the broomstick silhouette less than inspiring. The 1900's woman had no problems, the 'pigeon breast' was a requirement in clothing.

In the early 1900's America was welcoming immigrants by the thousands, and all were filled with hope. In some ways this cheerful outlook transferred itself to fashion.

The covert skirt and shirtwaist which was a carry over from the 1890's could be worn again and again and interchanged. The mail order catalogues of the 1900's are filled with types of lady's waists, some of them in practical wool flannel. We tend to want to collect the things of rare beauty in clothing and much of what we have left to us is just that, but the ordinary day wear has a homey, well made look and often tells us more about the people and their lifestyles than the more lavish examples. While prices are rising astronomically on the elaborate dresses and gowns, they are going up more slowly on the lesser examples, but going up they are.

The average woman was a practical soul and oftentimes had a real need to buy garments which would give long service. The small standing collar introduced in the 1890's was an integral part of the 1900's scene. 'Wool tricot' was a newly introduced fabric in 1902, the summer dresses were two piece white lawn and were very attractive with their lace, embroidery and ribbon trim. Prices ranged from $3.75 to $6.75, not inexpensive for the time. We tend to think of that period as always incorporating the high banded neckline but the summer frocks were just as apt to be off the shoulder. With the popular bouffant hairdo tied at the nape with the large bows, these styles were quite alluring. Silk waists were expertly made and considered an absolutely necessary part of the wardrobe.

The young children and girls wore carbon copies of the adult clothing except for length which could vary from 20 to 28 inches in children one to five years old. Sailor type waists were in vogue for girls up to 14 years but the wide collar over the shoulder was prevalent.

Men were encased in one or three button cutaway frock coats or the single or double breasted sack which is a straight-lined jacket, and the average width of the pants leg was 22 inches at bottom. It was a neat look, a dandified look, worn with a bowler hat and high collar with bow tie. Surprisingly, many heavy overcoats from that period survive.

They can be found in differing lengths from 42 inches to 52 inches, depending on the height of the wearer, but the 42 inch coat was generally worn short, at knee length.

The cane was standard, and today we see an occasional good cane collection, but overall there are relatively few people collecting them. The umbrellas and canes of the 1900's are quite neglected by the general collecting public. The variety is vast and can keep a collector busy for years. The various material with which the handles were made are endlessly intriguing and often outlasted the cane or umbrella itself. Today we see these relics in the jewelry cases of dealers, and the sterling silver tops are already the subject of serious consideration.

Boys and younger men wore 3 piece suits for dress, consisting of coat, vest and knee pants which were tight fitting and usually made with 'double knees'. These met high stockings at the knee.

It should be remembered that men's clothing can be striking and expertly made, but currently it is largely the province of museums and costume departments of colleges and threatrical companies. Boys and men's clothing beautifully round out a diarama or a family scene of manikins. Not too many collectors have ventured into this field, except for some of the accessories like hats and caps, and this market is bound to make serious price gains.

One of the most important things a serious collector of Vintage Clothing must consider is display. Toward this, it is important to buy older dress forms if possible. If collecting before 1940 is your main focus, buy any dress form you see. In a one dimensional setting the bustle or the train, for example, do not show to advantage, but on a dress form all these details are immediately apparent. Here, of course, you compete with many small retailers who are also looking for these forms as elegant display pieces.

The older forms are usually marked with the manufacturer's name and dated, and these are greatly coveted, as are the old wicker which are a challenge to find, the type which can be made small or large, and the ones with iron bases. But buy any form you see until you can buy exactly what you want, so your wonderful old clothes will avoid creasing, folding, and general wear and tear when you take them out to show.

41

The old wooden hat forms make marvelous background for hats of the period. It is difficult to show a hat collection properly unless the shape and detail can be appreciated and for this you need a hat stand. Although I have uncovered no very large collections of stands, smaller ones abound, and since dealers themselves need them if they carry hats, they are not scarce but getting harder to find.

Nothing is more beautiful than a hat collection nicely set out, it can be used instead of sculpture, in many ways that is what a well mounted hat resembles. Hats are colorful and different and are a surprising aid to decor.

Some of the hatstands shown in this guide have been found at flea markets and the smaller shops and for the clothing collector it is important to keep in touch with these sources. Some remarkably lovely clothing is turning up this way and recently I purchased a pair of 1920's silk lounging pajamas for much less than the going rate. Basically though, the collector in this field needs to have rapport with a dealer in fine vintage fashion who will supply the kinds of garments in which you are most interested, in good condition.

Decorators, in a sense, are also seeking clothing and accessories of earlier periods to be used to accent a room, and you will find competition from people who have no interest in vintage clothing but have an eye for the unusual. Such a couple has an old life-size corset form, out of a mid-western store, ornamenting their living room. As with all artifacts concerned with vintage clothing, it is a conversation piece. So the clothing collector needs to buy whatever is pertinent to the collection when it is available, this is such a fast-growing field the watchword is haste.

Recently, an exquisite Edwardian silk dress became available through an estate sale. In perfect condition, the price was high. The skirt consisted of much precious material which seemed to flow from a bodice which was boned, but the collector hesitated. After considering it for a few hours, she decided to buy it, but it had been sold. Not too long after, the gown which had the typically low decolletage was spotted at a downtown shop at an even higher price, and it was marked 'sold'.

This is becoming an increasing problem as well as a great boon to the private collector, as more and more shops devoted to Vintage Fashion open and competition becomes keener. It is to the dealer in fine old clothing that the collector should turn for fashions of the Edwardian period. Although the typical dresses and suits are easily recognized, some of the other apparel made between 1900 and 1910 is not so characteristic and it takes a trained eye to identify it. With enough experience, collectors will acquire the same skill.

The Edwardian age fostered a fashion which has never actually disappeared. The shirtwaist look in a modified way has continued to this very day, largely because it is a flattering and easy style. Fashion was still set by the wealthy in 1900-1910 and Paris reigned supreme.

At the turn of the century women wore sweeping skirts and since they did, literally, sweep the floor it must have been a monumental chore to keep clothing immaculate. Around the house, some women resorted to large bands of material folded over the hem and secured on both sides.

Crossing streets and climing stairs called for lifting the skirt and it was important to do this correctly so as not to disturb the fit over hip and back.

Worth, the incomparable designer and trend setter was still a famous name and for the fashionable a gown from Worth of Paris was elegance personified.

Furs and feathers, as well as umbrellas and parasols, were part of the costume.

Magazines of that time show innumerable ads for underthings and corsets which were considered part of a bride's trousseau and were an important part of the fashionable life of the female. One of the adjuncts to fashion which should appeal to any collector is the boudoir cap which was worn to cover any less than perfect coiffure. These were made in a wide range of materials and trimmings, and are among the delightful fripperies one can search for. While still relatively inexpensive because they have been neglected for a long time, they are rising in price.

Since there are still not too many collectors of these delightful concoctions it is a relatively untapped field, but now their beauty and potential is recognized and a beginning collector should waste no time. About 5 years ago, I purchased a lovely little silk and crocheted cap for $6, recently I saw a similar cap for almost 6 times that. From an investment standpoint, that is certainly appreciation.

During parts of the Edwardian years, shoes were not always visible, as time went on and skirts shortened, the shoe again became somewhat important. Vintage shoes are becoming expensive and any from this period either high buttoned or high laced are quickly sold. The more utilitarian shoes, which were high laced, are almost impossible to distinguish from a man's shoe. Before I began my consuming pursuit of vintage fashion, I bought a pair of what I thought must surely be a man's footwear. A little research showed this to be a woman's shoe, so beware if you are new to period.

It is always wise to look for shoes of the same vintage as the garment, so that when you display you can accompany the dress or suit with the complementary accessories. This gives a sense of completeness, and a sense of history.

The Hobble skirt was prevalent in the years before the first World Ware, satin shoes for evening and high button shoes for day wear. The flippant "that went out with high button shoes" summed up the reaction of the following decades to that style and that may be why they are so difficult to find. But the shoe collector has a veritable bonanza of choices. Patent leather vamps paired with elegant uppers, sometimes silk or suede, are just waiting somewhere to be discovered.

Of all the collectibles in clothing, shoes seem to attract the fewest fans, although a New York Department store recently had a rather limited showing of vintage designer shoes. Shoes are one of the great indicators of prevailing fashions and often delineate a specific era even more than the garments. Home sewing became widely practiced in the early part of the 20th century and so some fashions could have been made in older styles or clothing could have been altered, but shoes would normally have to be purchased regularly and would thus have been made in the prevailing mode and each time had its typical footwear.

The collector hopes for a pair that is unworn, but this is not always possible, and even museums are now resigned to showing shoes that are in less than perfect condition. High button shoes, especially those belonging to small children have an endearing quality that shoes of other periods do not possess, and of course there are those shoe button hooks which come in several sizes and have attractive handles, often silver or mother-of-pearl. Try for a few of these to match the shoes. Try always to think of your collectible in the round; the shoe button for the right shoe style; the appropriate stand for the hat; the dress form to show off the gown; the correct handbag, all of these can give meaning to your clothing. Visit your local museum or an available Vintage Clothing Museum (such museums are proliferating rapidly) or even a fine Vintage Clothing shop to see how the professionals do it. Any collection benefits from being complete and it is the small things which lend interest. The Smithsonian Institution is now placing emphasis on the background of the First Ladies' gowns. As well as the gowns themselves, the display is moving to include period rooms and accessories.

The hats had to be spectacular to accommodate the coiffure, and a long hatpin was needed. Hatpins are an almost legendary collectible and are often classed with jewelry, but I feel that those who love the Edwardian era should collect a few representative hatpins. A simplistic rule of thumb has it that the older the hatpin the longer the shaft and this is usually true, after all it had to pierce hat, hair, rats, padding and heaven knows what else. Hatpins, which were costing only a few dollars a few years ago can now go for astronomical prices depending on age, the kind of metal used as well as the genuineness of the stones, and beauty.

Of special interest during the 1900-1910 period were the hats men wore. A man's hat, you may say, is just a hat. Not true, even today when hats are seldom worn, notice the caps men are donning with more frequency; baseball caps, caps with company logos, caps with club emblems, usually vented on top and back for summer comfort, and peaked. In warm areas of the country these caps are becoming commonplace. In 1900 the top hat went with the frock coat, the homburg was becoming necessary to the less formal day suit and the straw hat became the fancy of both men and women.

Just as the fashions of women have moved to the less formal, the coats and caps of the gentlemen who drove their motorcars were for those times, fairly informal. In fact, the motorcar was beginning to change America and Americans.

It was in 1913 that a revolutionary change altered women's clothing. It was the V-neck and we can only imagine the freedom that must have brought to the 1900's woman. It was avant-garde for the time and not everyone immediately rushed into it, and the shirtwaist and gored skirt persisted. Silk stockings were worn and on shirts of sheer batiste sparkled cyrstal or rhinestone buttons. Cotton voile was the choice for day dresses, it was dainty and figured, and lined in a "suitable color".

By 1915 skirts began to widen considerably at the hem but remained tight at the hips. The high waist, raised as much as 2½ inches above normal gave a long line to the skirt, and the voluptuous, mature ideal of the first decade of the 20th century was phasing out.

The years from 1900 to the outbreak of World War I were a time of extravagance and ostentation. The balloon sleeves of the 1890's disappeared and were now tight and extended halfway down the hand. The function of clothing was more practical, how could they have functioned in their overdone, elaborate clothing, as they left the home for shops and offices it was evident that clothing was going to have to adapt to the woman instead of woman adapting to the dictates of fashion.

It was this era that gave us the Gibson girl with the hour glass figure and we can probably forgive fashion arbiters for almost anything just for the pleasure of looking at her. Charles Dana Gibson's creation was the epitome of female beauty of her day, and so lovely that even now, with a few alterations, she can be considered the model for full-blown beauty. Her intricate pompadour coiffure, her gorgeous exposed shoulders by night and her trim fitting high neckline by day, coupled with her hour glass figure and provocative poses, decorate more walls of nostalgia buffs than one can count even in this jeans and tee-shirt age. One of the world's best kept secrets is the 'Gibson Man' but attractive as he was, he obviously didn't have that special something.

The late years of the decade were geared toward making the 'World Safe for Democracy'. Simple lines had replaced the former constricting clothing and by the time the men returned home from the trenches they must have suffered a culture shock — they had left a nation of females mincing about in long hobble skirts and and now found the vision of women in skirts just below the knee. Women who had participated in the war effort began to forsake the clothes which limited their activities. Realization had arrived that there were things to do, women could do them, but the garments had to fit the dream.

That war changed not only fashion, it changed the entire world forever.

What is fashion anyway? It is probably the ultimate manifestation of a basic need, to be warm, to impress, or as some anthropologists would have it, an early need to be better than the animals. Whatever it is, the clothing collector daily gives thanks.

The average woman has probably not often had the desire to be dressed by a great couturier. Indeed it would be superfluous to her way of life, so it has always been the leisured class which has made fashion. True, the designs filtered down so what we buy off the rack can certainly be traced to an original made in Paris, or Ireland, or Italy but there are hordes of women whose main aim is to look attractive and depending on the occasion, alluring or competent.

Men have been locked into the business type clothing for so long that today any changes taking place are influenced by Television. Men's cosmetics, colognes, high heeled boots, brighter colors — Louis the XIV would be right at home with the coming revolution in men's fashions. Some women are no doubt as startled to see these alterations in men's fashions as the returning service men were to see the short skirts of 1919, men have taken to the sports shirt and jacket and in many circles, academia is one, their is less emphasis on the tie; and the hat for purposes other than warmth, is a thing of the past.

Nineteen Twenty marked more than the end of a decade, the coiffure was beginning to sport the permanent wave, shorter skirts and more slender figures with a less defined waistline had somehow evolved. Women had the vote, they were moving into the workforce in numbers and their clothes were becoming less restricted and more utilitarian. It was a far cry from Women's Lib, but the signs were there, and as usual fashion foreshadowed the future.

1925 bridesmaid's dress, cape effect over sheer sleeves, value $155-165.

1926 bride and groom, ankle length sheer gauze dress, white hose, traditional veil with train. Wedding dresses of this era, $200-245. Tuxedo, black with satin lapels, $150-175.

Close up of bride and groom, 1912 wedding.

1912 wedding. Bride wears satin, lace and traditional veil with orange blossom headpiece and net train. Small ball fringe on dress yoke and sleeve edges. Chemisette of chiffon with high neck banded at top with small seed pearls. Dress, $850-1,000. Veil, $250-300. Bridesmaid, standing, satin dress, v-neck with lace insert, pearl and lace edging on cape. Dress, $650-750. All wear long kid gloves, $40-55 pair. Boy wears linen jacket and pants (white) $100-125. Mens' suits, wool, value, $125-$150.

Wedding photo. 1903. Bride wears sheer voile, pleated bodice with lace yoke. High banded collar. Fullness and small cape at top of sleeves. Brides dress has three ruffles and lace inset in skirt. Dress $1,500-2,000. Bridesmaid, left, sheer voile with ruffled skirt, large sleeve fullness and small cape effect at shoulder. Dress, $1,200-$1,500. Mens' suits, with vests, wool, value, $175-225.

Betty Luther modeling beige sheer wedding dress, 1910 — at Gold Diggers' Fashion Show, Oct. 1977, Medford, Or. Kenn Knackstedt, photographer.

1905 golfing and tennis costumes. The woman's outfit would probably be found as separates today and would fall into the price range quoted previously for 1900's blouses and skirts. This is also true of the gentleman's outfit, the pants would fall into the $35-45 range.

College graduating class, 1905. Woman's dress, $400-425. Gentlemen wear the high buttoned frock coat, vests with high rounded collars and importantly placed buttons, one wears striped trousers, notice the differing ties. Complete suits, $500-550.

Dandy of 1912, striped trousers, long jacket, pearl button vest, Small, rounded collar. Vest, $95-110. Jacket $65-85. Trousers, $75-85.

1918 Maternity wear, suits, each $350-400, if furred, $450-500. Hats, $110-135. Notice the footwear.

Formal gold dress with train. Trimmed with lace and jet beads and completely lined except for train. Yellow pearl buttons. Worn about 1900. Black lace ball fan. Value, dress, $300. Fan 75.

C. 1900. Silk Chiffon, "one of the fancy new materials" at the turn of the century. Dress, $500-600.

Calico morning dress or wrapper, c. 1900. Square collar, rounded yoke, ruffles at shoulder. Skirt has wide flounce at ankle. Made from a contemporary pattern. Value of original in period. $95-125. Photo Courtesy of FOLKWEAR, San Rafael, Ca.

C. 1915, striped cotton day dress, belt inset, brown and white, hand crocheted yoke. Value $125-145.

Left to right: Ladies' House dresses, 1916. Simple style, button front, small collar, bishop sleeves (plain at the shoulder and gathered into a cuff at the wrist.) Usually found in washable fabric. Value $135-155. Apron, serviceable work apron, front panel fitted, gingham, value $40-60. House dress, side closing waist, 7 gore skirt. Cotton. Value $135-155.

Costumes for home wear: 1915. Left: ladies' bath robe, flannel or wool. Not too many robes of this type survive. Value $45-65. Right: House dress, 2 piece, plain blouse with center front closing. Skirt has 3 gores and is gathered at the top, the sides and the back. These were usually made of washable material, and occasionally in wool. Value $55-75.

Morning wear. Left: one piece apron. Single piece, long seams at the sides, neck is a simple round, large arm holes. Usually found in calico or cambric or gingham. 1914. Value $30-40. Right: Ladies Kimono. Slender lines, panel front closing on its left side without fullness. Satin trim. 1914. Value $85-100.

Home garments: left to right: 1912. Semiprincess style, for home wear, sateen. $150-175. Child's apron. Sacque style, fastens in back, has ties extending from side seam, roll collar and long sleeves. Figured lawn. Value $65-85. House dress, morning wear. Has patch pocket and some sleeve fullness at shoulder. Cotton crepe. Value $150-175. Russian suit for young boy. Coat closes over at side standing collar, sleeves have little fullness and band cuff. Pants are made without a fly. Linen. Value $185-200. Maternity dress. This is attached to a lining which is adjustable. Drop shoulders and plain sleeves. Lightweight silk. Value $200-250.

Typical shirtwaist styles of the first decade of the 1900's. Value of each of the blouses: $150-175. Value of each of this type skirt. $125-150. Price depends on quality and trim.

C. 1900 gown. Handkerchief linen, inset linen. A magnificent dress. $400-450.

Detail of brown handkerchief linen dress.

1905 Gibson Girl silhouette and coiffure.
Outfit, $450-500.

1905 Young ladies' outfit, $150-175.

1905. All dresses and suits in this period and of these styles, unless they have some unusual features are priced at $350-400, but prices at this time vary from shop to shop and area to area. All prices on clothing of this period are rising very rapidly.

Charles Stevens & Bros. advertisement, 1905. Coats of this kind, large sleeves and 50 inches long should range between $400-500. Hat on left, $55-75 in excellent condition. Hat on right, $55-75 in excellent condition.

The rather plain jackets should range between $175 and $225. The wrap with its extra large armholes for the large sleeve is a very desirable item. Wraps of this type range between $350-400, again depending on materials, condition and trim.

Shirtwaists of this type should range between $150-200 depending on materials, workmanship and trim.

Jacquard silk with French lace revers, appliqued embroidery, French rosettes, mauve with purple velvet sash, square buttons. C. 1910, value $175-225. Woman's straw hat, c. 1910, $45-65.

This is the stylish overblouse effect, 1916. The skirt is circular and the girdle is wide satin. Value $395-425. Chemise tunic dress, tunic is one unbroken piece from shoulder to hem. Neck has a turnover collar at back and sides, cheviot. Value $395-425.

L. to R. Afternoon wear, 1915. Shirtwaist dress. Waist has cape falling from collar in back, pointed sleeve edges, belted. Value $235-250. Lower skirt section of this dress is velvet, over skirt is satin, silk waist with lace jacket and velvet sash. Value $325-375. This wool coat was intended for a younger lady. Considered a practical rather than decorative garment and worn over a gored skirt. Coat value, $135-150. Blouse with stand up collar is worn under bolero, extremely popular in 1915. Overskirt matches bolero. Value $350-400.

Left to right: Everyday dresses, winter, 1915.
Shirtwaist dress, printed crepe de chine, high
neck with gathers. Skirt is of mixed cheviot.
Value $345-375. Raglan sleeve blouse with
tunic skirt. Matching underskirt. Value $300-
350. The popular overblouse, worn with long
sleeved waist. Tunic skirt. Chiffon, silk and
satin trim. Value $400-450.

2 piece dress, 1915. Overblouse
and girdle with an underblouse of
satin with frilled neckline. Velvet
and satin. Value $350-400. Coat,
loose sports coat or 'college coat'.
Sacque cut (which means without a
break from the shoulder to the
hem. Value $200-250.

Misses' dresses, 1915. Considered a youthful style, this blouse and skirt has a bordered skirt and a blouse whose collar can be worn flat or arranged to close in high necked style. Sleeve fullness is gathered into the band cuff. Skirt has a deep round at the front. Serge. Value $175-200. Right: Overblouse worn with a plain waist, which again has a convertible neck. Bishop sleeves with wide cuff. Skirt, 2 piece, circular cut. Usually found in fine serge with chiffon or net, or velvet and wool. Value $175-200. Today it is difficult to determine that these were worn by young women since the sizes are large.

Ladies suits, 1915. This coat-suit boasts a jacket of the latest 1915 style. It extends over the hips, and has a front center closing. Revers and small collar, patch pockets under the lap of these passes the narrow belt. Skirt is four gored and quite a bit of ankle showing is permitted with this style. Corduroy. $400-450. Ladies' dress. High standing collar, overblouse has yoke effect, skirt is circular cut which closed in center front. Satin and net $450-475. Furs were often worn with this type garment, either around the neck or a muff as shown.

Afternoon dresses, 1913. Frock for young girl. Light and dark fabric, buttons down front, five gored skirt. Value $285-300. One piece Empire dress. Striped silk. Value $300-325. Shirtwaist costume of tan cotton pongee with white line collar and cuffs. Value $285-300. White serge afternoon dress, black satin trim, value $325-350.

Fall, 1913. L. to R. Box coat, cut on raglan lines, worn with simple, tailored skirt. Coat, value $150-175. Walking dress: Plain blouse opens over a vest insert. Skirt is four gore. A walking dress was considered utilitarian, ideal for marketing, shopping or exercise. 1913. Value $300-325. Street dress to be worn without a coat. The dress has a coat-blouse effect with a 2 gore skirt. 1913. Value $300-325.

Another shirtwaist dress, 1913. Plain waist, striped, unusual sleeve which continues to point to the edge of the collar. Skirt is four gore, closing at the left side of the back, belted. Usually these waists are made of pongee silk and skirts of light woolen goods, serge or cheviot. Value $250-275. Young girl's dress: 2 piece skirt with tunic over overdress. Wide panels front and back and belted. Linen, value $100-135. Cream serge dress, 1913. Bodice is deep U filled in with a yoke of lace and moire taffeta. Skirt narrows at ankle. Value $300-325. Plain waist and skirt, shirtwaist type. Neckline trimmed with notched collar and is closed in the duchesse style in the center front. Skirt closes in the front. Waist is Japanese silk with satin trim. Silk sash. Value $295-325.

Suits from 1913. Three quarter length coat, 2 piece skirt. Sleeves have a little fullness at the shoulder. 2 piece skirt is plain at top and can be found in raised or regulation waistline. These suits are difficult to find. Value $350-375.

2nd from left: a semi-tailored calling gown, popular in Paris when something "plain" was called for. The coat which is cutaway in front discloses a vest, and has a little fullness at each side. Skirt has 3 gores. Value $350-375. For hard usage, including "business" this was the type preferred. The coat falls well below the hips and fastens below the waistline. 2 piece skirt absolutely plain. Value $300-325.

Afternoon dresses, 1913. Waistline at almost natural level. Left, satin dress with draped skirt and jacket effect over chiffon chemisette. Tight sleeves. Value $400-450. Afternoon dress. Draped skirt revealing underskirt of silk to match silk jacket and lining of dress. Dress has double line of buttons decorating front. Value $400-450.

Left to right: House dress, lawn with belt and panel at bottom of skirt of chiffon. Matching cap. Value of dress, $200-225; cap, $45-55. Street dress, drop shoulder plain blouse, high waisted 3 gore skirt joined to waist with girdle. Value $225-275. Street dress, shirtwaist, $275-295. All 1912-1913.

Afternoon gowns. Left to right: C. 1910. Calling costume, 2 piece, blouse is gathered along the shoulder seam in the front and the fullness thus falls loosely about the figure. It is gathered at the belt. V-neck which could be filled with a small chemisette and standing collar. 2 piece skirt fits snugly but at the lower opening of the side seam there is a slit which displays the petticoat. Value $275-325. 2 pieces. The blouse is gathered along the shoulder seam in front and along the lower edge of a shoulder yoke in back, which gives a soft, droopy effect. The skirt is a plain, peg top style with a little fullness in front but the back is flat in the upper part with a bulge below the hips then again flattens. Recommended for a slender or medium figure. $300-325.

3rd from left: For morning wear. Bodice built on shirtwaist lines but is given a decorative touch by the very low drop shoulder and the yoke which is straight and is used only in front. Sleeve is plain at the shoulder but wide at the armhole where it is set in and slightly full where it joins the cuff at the wrist. Narrow skirt with sash. Morning wear demanded simplicity. Value $250-275. 4th from left: For the Matinee of Afternoon Tea. Plain blouse opens in front, skirt has three gores which gives a seamless back and a center-front closing. Value $295-350. Two models wear high button shoes, two wear pumps with buckles.

Spring 1913. Evening dresses, left to right: Collarless neck has a plaiting of chiffon, and velvet bow. Banding embellishes the frock. Value $325-350. Cream voile with white lace collar and yoke and heavy cream lace embellishments. Draped skirt with pearl ornament. Value $500-600. Waist closes at front, skirt is a one piece empire model with tunic. Revers on skirt of gold satin, with tiny gilt buttons. Value $400-450.

Maternity blouses and 'coatees', 1917-1918.
Values: top row, left to right: $25-35; $30-40.
Center; $35-40.
2nd row left to right; $30-40; $30-40.
Bottom row, left to right; $25-35; $25-35.

1918 Blouse. The back of the blouse extends over the shoulders to meet the lightly gathered front and gathers at the back center waist into a self-tie or ribbon which encircles the waist to tie in front. Deep rectangular neckline. Made from contemporary pattern. Value of original, $85-95.

'Armistice Blouse'. Lightly gathered front with long collar falling softly over a center panel or 'vestee'. Made from a contemporary pattern by Folkwear. Value of original $95-125. Photo courtesy Folkwear, San Raphael, Ca.

Short jacket, white silk with black applique, standing collar, c. 1900. Value $250-300.

Jacket, c. 1900. Faille with passementerie and lace edged sleeves lined and neckline decorated with stemmed flowers, and leaves. Value $250-300. Back and front views.

Handmade blouse, c. 1900. Four varieties of hand made lace, 3/4 sleeves, tight wrists, handkerchief linen. $400-450.

Blouse-jacket, taffeta, blue cream and black stripes, worn in 1900. Value $175-200.

1906. Blouses of this type: depending on condition, fabric, and detail range $195-250; hats of this year should cost between $100-150, again depending on material and trim.

Camisole, c. 1900, the bodice of the camisole boasts tucks and lace inserts. Fitted in back, bloused in front. Closes with drawstrings at neckline and waist. $95-115. Value of original. Photo courtesy Folkwear, San Rafael, Ca. Gored petticoat has dust ruffle at hemline, drawstring waist ties at back. Value of original, $100-120. Knee length drawers gathered at the curved waistband, front gusset and 2 buttoned side plackets. Ruffles at knee. Value of original $125-135.

Bloomers attached to camisole top, c. 1915-1919. Value $55-75.

Women's underthings: Left, c. 1915-1916 'teddy', Silk. A 'teddy' is a camisole top and loose panties, combined in one garment. The 'teddy' shown is hand made and hand embroidered. Value $55-60. Right: slip, c. 1920, silk, hand embroidered. Value $50-55.

1916. On left is a negligee gown. Plain sacque cut from shoulder to hem, apron front and back, hand scalloped trim. Found in various materials. Value $125-175. Maternity gown. Laced in front with darts which makes it adjustable. Skirt is one piece gathered at top with small frill. Found in various materials. Value $100-150. Combination corset-cover and short petticoat. Corset cover fastens in back. Short petticoat fits tightly. Lawn. Value corset cover, $55-75. Garment intact, $100-125. Petticoat, short, $35-50.

Graduation dress of 1908. White, elaborately detailed with embroidered netting. Value $300-345.
Photo by Douglas R. Smith. Courtesy of Southern Oregon Historical Society.

Misses' dresses, 1912. Left to right: Designed for the high school girl, this frock is rose cashmere. Middy style with sailor collar. Unusual lacing. Value $250-285. Middy dress, blouse is joined to a 6 gored skirt. Belt and sailor collar. Serge. Value $275-300. This dress closes at the left side of the front and has a 2 piece skirt. Cashmere, value $275-300. Lingerie dress. Embroidered flouncing with the yoke formed of rows of insertion with fine lawn. Organdy. Value $350-375.

Gymnasium suits for young misses in 1913. Left, regulation type, plain blouse with round neck and small collar. Bloomers are separate and of moderate fullness. Lighweight flannel. Set value, $150-155. Blouse, $35-45. Bloomers, $75-85. Right: Same suit for the older girl, v-neck and pocket with striped sailor collar and sleeve edges. Value, set, $150-155. Blouse, $50-60. Bloomers, $75-85.

Young ladies' wear is often sold as adult clothing even though it was shorter and the skirt was more boxy than the preferred ladies' gored type. Sizes were ordinarily 14 to 18 so again the waistline could have rivaled an adult waist. The look is different, much less fitted and looser. This sort of costume is very difficult to find, the range for the dresses would be $150-175 and the suits $165-185. The coats are again identifiable by the sleeve at the shoulder, and the rather high back strap. $145-165.

1913. For school or play. The large bow at front waist line distinguishes this dress. Gingham. $95-115. This dress is for the very young child in which there is more interest at the moment than in clothing for older children. This affects prices. Wide box pleat down the front and back wide collar. Belted. Value $100-115. Sacque cut, front cut with deep U and filled in with a laced chemisette with collar. Cashmere. Value $100-135.

Body and sleeves of this coat are one piece. Belted. Wool. Value $95-115. Girls' dress. Copied from a new fashion for women in the winter of 1913, the deep, straight yoke. A row of shirring at the waist, and over this a wide belt. Plaid silk with velvet trim. Value $125-150. School dress for winter. Serge value, $95-115.

Summer frocks, 1913. Diagonal front closing, wide shawl collar ending at belt which has buttons below, linen. Value $135-145. Seamless shoulder in drop style, ribbon threaded through for effect, cotton. Value $100-110. Bodice ad skirt dress. Simple style with wide banding trim. Skirt joins waist beneath belt, cambric. Value $95-110.

1913. Waist and skirt dress for young girl. Skirt attaches to waist beneath the sash. Cotton. Value $95-125. Russian dress worn by boy. Plain sacque cut, closes at side, sleeves now showing no fullness at shoulder. Usually worn by boys under three years of age. Value $125-150. Gingham dress in tan stripes. Value $85-110. Sacque cut, one piece. Hand embroidered collar and cuffs, belt passes through slots. Value $125-150. One piece, broad belt, hand embroidered. Linen. Value $125-145.

1913. Dresses for the small girl. Long bloused effect, pleated skirt, bow at neck, button front. Cotton. Value $95-125. One piece dress with attached bloomers. Green challis with rosette of blue satin at side. Value $95-125. One piece with front closing and separate guimpe. Value $100-135. School coat. Box style, circular front, contrasting trim. Value $135-145. Utility dress made in many washable materials as well as wool. Value $95-125. Embroidered flouncing on this one piece dress. Closes at back. Value $135-165. Large bows if original, $30-40.

Boys' single breasted overcoat. Well fitting collar and rolled lapels. Usually found in wool. 1913. $85-100.

1915. Children's coat. Plain sacque coat with a highly ornamental cape. Round neck is trimmed with a small collar and the full sleeves end in a cuff. Value $125-150. Often these children's coats were made in expensive materials such as ottoman silk, velvet, cashmere, fur. The bonnet, which went with this kind of coat was also usually silk or velvet, is round and full, finished with a flat band around the head. Value $45-55.

1915. Sacque cut, shirring at neck and waist for children up to 6 years of age. Challis. Value $95-125. Long waisted blouse with pleated skirt. Collars and cuffs match hem border. Belt. Value $100-115. Tunic over waist and skirt. Belt of leather at low waistline. Tunics were also popular with the ladies of 1915. Value $110-145. Sailor dress with collar which joins revers with notches. Pleated skirt. Cashmere. $135-165.

1915. Girls' apron. One piece with a short dart below arm to adjust to figure. Closes in back. Gingham. $30-40. Girls' coat. Simple box type, raglan sleeves. Tweed. Value $65-85. Boys' overcoat, with long shoulder-cape which does not cover coat buttons in front. Detachable cape. Wool. Value with cape $150-175. Coat without cape, $95-125. Cap in child's size, $25-35.

For the small child, 1915. Top left. Garment is quite simple, front side closing. Square neck, can be worn by boy or girl. Serge but can be found in velveteen. Value, $95-135. Boys' Russian dress. Wool, high neck with banded collar, closing well over to side in front. $95-150. Simple dress with plain blouse with drop shoulder and wide collar. Diagonal closing across front and meets line of skirt closing. Value $100-145. Boy's suit. Coat of modified Eton type, edges meet at neck but hang apart to hem of jacket which ends below the hips. Vest and trousers made without a fly. Velveteen. Value $175-195. Slip type dress with guimpe. Small box pleats front and back. Dress with belt. $95-125.

Top, girls' coat, high neck, small collar, circular skirt. Wool. Value $135-155. Left, made of different materials which was considered 'new' in 1916. Serge top with velvet skirt. Value $135-155. Separate skirt and blouse, which is long length. Satin with wool. Value $135-155.

C. 1916. Cotton with lace dress. $40-45.

INFANTS' and CHILDREN'S COATS.

Infants and children's coats, 1917-18. Values, left to right, top row: Cashmere coat, long; value, $100-125; short, value $95-110. Cashmere coat, long, value $100-125; short, value $95-110. Crepetella coat, long, value $100-125; short, value $95-110. Cape with hood all three types, value $75-95. Or these can be considered as all falling within the ranges listed. Bottom row: left to right: chinchilla: $135-150; velveteen corduroy: $50-70; gabardine: $45-65; velveteen corduroy, brown: $50-70; quilted coat lining: $28-38; quilted sateen coat lining: $20-30; quilted silk coat lining: $25-35; chinchilla coat: $135-150.

Children's short dresses, 1917. Values, top row, left to right: $35-40; $30-40; $45-50; $40-50; $45-50; $40-50; $40-45. Values, bottom row, left to right: All of these garments are in the $35-65 range.

Child's (boy's) dress. White cotton, scalloped. Worn in 1914. Value $45-50.

Children's clothing of 1906. Boys clothing has not reached the levels of girls' clothing, and there seems to be less of it available. Children's wear of this era and of the types shown range between $135-150.

Long, cambric infant's baptismal dress, worn by boy, 1900, hand made, standing collar. Value $100-135.

Boy's suit, blue serge, paneled front, 2 piece. Bow of linen. C. 1900. Value $75-125.

C. 1905-1910. Large plumed hat, $110-145. Silk afternoon dress, lace collar, value $195-225. Metallic beaded bag with sterling silver frame, engraved with initials and decorated with long fringe. Value $155-175.

Three different versions of the crocheted boudoir cap and different varieties of the hat stand.

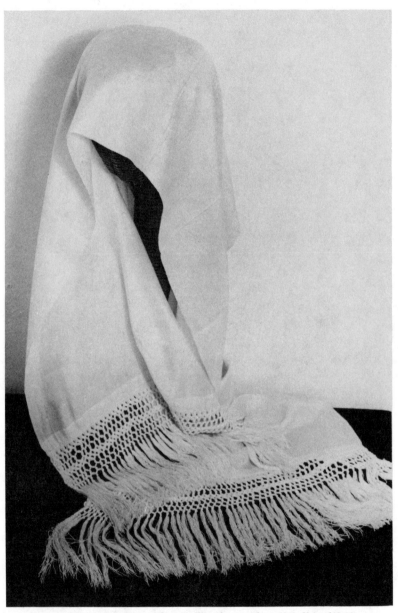

Creamy white pongee silk scarf, heavily fringed, worn about 1910. Value $85-95.

CHAPTER III
1920 - 1940

No wonder we are dazzled by the 1920's. A time in the United States when triumphant post war fever swept the land, it was a time to release tension, a time to let go. Americans were having the last big fling, althought they didn't know it. There was more freedom for women and the entire attitude was young. Women bobbed their hair, did the frenzied Charleston and listened to jazz. The evening clothes reflected the outlook, it was easy, it sparkled and it was a trifle bizarre.

The flapper leaped out of every page. Mention the word today and a vision of pencil thin, bobbed haired beauty, wearing her rather shapeless beaded dress and long colored beads comes instantly to mind. She also wore cloche hats, although later in the decade hats became large and lovely, and her waistline was only suggested by bands near the hip line. In truth many of the dresses of this period can be found in rather large sizes so not everyone was petite. The style was generally flattering to the figure, being basically straight line and loose.

The hair and the hats were prominent fashion features in the 20's. The cloche was it. Tightly moulded to the head, sometimes with a narrow brim, it was worn well down on the forehead. It was made of felt, silk, velvet, satin or crepe and it complemented the dresses beautifully. The individual touches on the hats were enchanting — "a brilliant pin placed on the right front side", or "a peaked cloche of capuchine crepe satin trimmed with long feathered bands which break into soft tufts at the apex".

"Millinery", said a prominent 1920's magazine, "is not just making hats, no indeed. Millinery in its creation is an art." It was, and is, true that the proper headpiece considers facial contours, skin and hair coloring, and the coiffure will frame the face in a flattering way. Also the proper hat can strike a master stroke for individuality. Coordinated properly with the dress or suit it is that last finishing touch.

Plain silk frocks decorated with colored silk flowers, or 3 sprays of silk roses with silver encrusted leaves and flexible stems on a rustling taffeta dress might match the spray of flowers on the hat. The flowers on the hats were made of silk or chiffon or sheer gauze. The lapel flower made an appearance at this time and has never entirely deserted the fashion scene since.

The cloche hat survived into the 1930's but it did not continue to dominate the 20's scene; by 1926 large brims were the rage. But time was running out on the hat industry. During the early 20's many thousands were employed in the hat industry in New York alone. What has happened to all those hats and elegant headgear of the 1920's? It seems to be one of the most difficult of periods from which to find good representative millinery but when such a piece is found it is usually a gem.

121

The beading on the evening dresses make these garments the goal of every 1920's vintage clothing collector, and often are sought by collectors of clothing of other periods. Not only is the workmanship superb, the beads glittering and worked into intricate designs, but the dresses are still eminently wearable if found in good condition.

Some are so heavily beaded that care must be taken in their display. Hangers are unsuitable and if a dress form is not available, the dress should be folded and stored carefully. Ready-made beaded panels could be bought separately and added to the basic slip-like dress.

Today, long after the heyday of these glamorous gowns, any collector of vintage fashion would be delighted to add one to a collection, and even non-collectors covet them. Today, everyone seems to love this fashion.

Displayed on a dress form the dresses seem to have a life of their own, they shimmer and change colors in different light and aside from their obvious beauty this may also be part of their appeal. The satins and chiffons move with every breeze. Sequins were also used generously in the late 20's as the curved and pointed irregular hemlines began to inch downward. Waist lines were still low on the hips, long dangling earrings were clearly visible with the short hair, and in evening wear the keynote was a kind of casual elegance.

In fact fashion arbiters were advising 'the studied, careless look'. "Avoid a dressy look, even in formal clothes," they said, and had some words of wisdom for the young college miss. "The college girl should wear felt hats, dented here and there nonchalantly, soft, pull-on gloves sufficiently large to crush generously, plain sandals or pumps, and all of this will create the well groomed but studied careless air that in this year of 1924 is really chic." Today's college girl would swoon at the thought, but when you find a 20's look hat that is dented here and there, it is more likely by design than accident.

Suits with matching frocks and a 3/4 matching coat were fine for street wear or a 3/4 length blouse of material to match the coat and worn with a tight skirt, was considered more than acceptable and the slightly mannish look of the earlier 20's was passing. The ensemble idea was stressed and capes were being worn again. Masculine type lounging robes were being worn by women and wide leather belts worn low on the hips were the big accessories.

The beaded bags which these lovelies carried already have so many devotees, it is probably sufficient to remark on their workmanship and beauty. It is rather late to begin such a collection because prices have risen steeply and continue upward. Already there exist many large collections of these, but if beaded bags are your fancy they are a beautiful investment.

The young people who danced all night in their fancy satin shoes were lively to the point of exhaustion. Our essential national innocence had been dissipated by the 'war to end all wars' and in the 20's the accent was on youth, 'flaming youth'. The flapper became a by-word.

John Held Jr. created her and named her 'flapper', so the story goes, because she often wore galoshes with the buckles undone and they flapped as she walked. Whatever the exact origin of the word, its two small syllables sum up an entire era.

Until recently the rental companies dealing in vintage clothing had few flapper types to loan. Not too long ago a college student friend sought in vain for a beaded dress, proper shoes and a feathered headband to wear to a school dance. Finally she borrowed the dress seen on page 143 from a private collector. It was such a success and elicited so many inquiries the collector now rents her clothing to selected customers. Business is brisk. She feels that she is educating the public, many of whom have never seen such clothing, especially the young people. Anyone with a good vintage clothing collection should definitely share it in some way with others, club meetings, junior groups of young people, convalescent homes, even schools. That is the ultimate joy of collecting; the sharing.

The girlish look of the early 1920's, reinforced by the soft materials used in the dresses, contrasted sharply with some of the movie stars of the day, personified by Pola Negri and her 'vamp' image. Other Hollywood stars held out against bobbing their hair, but the late Gloria Swanson was an early convert. This indecision about image was reflected in hem lengths which varied from knee length to calf length to almost ankle length.

Coco Chanel came along with her classic look that still retains a measure of popularity, and it is felt that in her the 20's spawned one of the great dress designers.

The short dresses of the early 20's led to more interest in the shoe. The Louis heeled, long pointed vamp, and T-strap pumps were entirely visible beneath the uneven hemlines of points or fringe.

For collectors shoes can show some wear if it does not affect the material of the uppers. Perfection is always the goal, but in the search for shoes this becomes very difficult. Proof of the fact that even some party clothes were worn often by the average person is the wear often found on the shoes of the 1920's. The shoes are intriguing though, and anyone collecting in this period needs at least one or two pairs to delineate the dress.

The shoe buckles are even more fun. Four years ago cut steel buckles could be bought for $4 or $5, and two years ago I paid $8 to $12 a pair. Recently prices have moved into the $30-$45 range. Although I have seen collections of buckles which are singles, it is wiser to search out the pairs. The values will hold and of course, it's necessary if they are to be worn unless you are a real trend setter and are willing to wear a different buckle on each shoe.

Although the cut steel are usually fine quality the rhinestone sets can be spectacular, but are somewhat more difficult to find. Often the backings are made of velvet, or satin, or patent leather, although some were made without any backing at all.

Shoe buckles can be traced to the Celts (600 B.C.) and since those ancient days their popularity has waxed and waned but never completely disappeared. There is tremendous variety in shoe buckles and their charm is a decided asset to a clothing collection. Recently at auction a pair of cut steel buckles in their original box sold for $75. We collectors are certainly on the right track.

And just what is happening in the auction market? Some larger auction houses are holding sales geared only to vintage clothing and interest is always high.

Furs seems to hold a special appeal for collectors who buy them not only to display but to wear. Recently a full length ocelet coat with a narrow mink trim sold for $4,000 at auction. This is a tremendous rise over a similar coat on which I had bid about 4 years ago.

Furs must be previewed very carefully since the small splits which develop as the fur dries out cannot always be noticed in a casual perusal.

The reason for this clamor for vintage furs is three-fold: 1. Their usefulness, 2. their scarcity, not only as vintage clothing but because many animals which were used to make those furs are now on endangered species lists and so the fur piece can never be duplicated. 3. luxury, the feeling that wearing an elegant fur coat imparts cannot be explained fully, but if you've never worn a vintage fur, try it, you'll like it. Another consideration is that the older fur coats are unusual bargains, oftentimes many hundreds of dollars less expensive than they were originally.

The velvet shown on page 149 is a perfect example. Where today could a coat of such quality and beauty be bought for the price quoted, where today could one buy a coat with such style and flair? Made in the 1920s it is flattering to the figure, the color is exquisite and anyone lucky enough to own it could hardly avoid a feeling of glamour. Isadora Duncan may or may not have worn it, but it certainly brings her to life.

The vintage clothing collector of the 1920's period should follow the general advice of dating within a decade unless historical research demands pinpointing. However, quite specific changes makes some years easily definable.

1920 women wore deeply crowned hats, the skirt was at ankle length or a bit shorter, the beltline was at the hip, long sleeves were tight and wrist length. The exposed leg cried out for slinky silk stockings and the beaded necklace became almost a badge.

In 1923-24 the cloche hat vied with the large organza or 'garden party' type, dresses were mid-calf length and rising, shoes had the Louis heels which were used throughout the 20's and the shoes themselves could be made of satin, kid or leather. The hip belt was still in fashion.

1925-1926. The big news was the hemline, now knee length. Women wore bust flatteners and girdles and fancy underwear. Petticoats or slips in beautifully detailed silk with narrow shoulder straps and lace and embroidered trim. These were worn short, well above the knee. It is mostly these slips and petticoats and the silk lounging pajamas which entice collectors today. The materials are fine, the workmanship exquisite and some are so elegant that they can be used today. At a recent party in New York a guest was wearing heavy silk lavender lounging pajamas under a silver fox jacket. The costume created a minor sensation. The undergarments should be a highly specialized collecting area. There are enough of them available to build a good collection without too much effort and they require less care than the gowns.

A minor revolution occured in the 1927-1929 period. The V-neckline was introduced and created controversy. The T strap shoe and cloche hat was still worn and generally there was a crossover of all styles.

By the 1920's it should be remembered that the made-to-order clothing catalogues were advertising ready to wear outfits for one and all. Now people could look beyond their Sunday best or 'company' outfit and indulge themselves with full wardrobes without too much expense and bother. This applied to the clothing of men and children as well as women. A large variety of styles and types were offered and the choices offered are reflected in the many 1920's garments we can now choose from.

Although all periods are reflected by the way people dress, the clothing of the 1920's is perhaps one of the most precise indicators of its time. It was an exciting decade, it had an air of forbidden fruit about it, it was a time of great changes and as the decade moved to its frantic close, economic barometers were predicting disaster.

If you are already a collector, or thinking of collecting clothes from the 20's try for a reputable dealer who handles only the best quality. Such a person will assure that your dress' beadwork is intact, the clothing clean, the hats have their original trim, appropriate shoes, and the furs soft and wearable; all the things that are important to the definitive collector who wishes to build a valuable, in depth collection.

Everybody today thinks back on the 1920's as a riotous time. For some, it surely was, but the millions who wore the ordinary clothing of the day are being neglected, their dresses and suits are interesting too. But everybody wants those beads.

Men of the 1920's were still in a conservative mood. The wide trousers were a change, sometimes they were as much as 22 to 24 inches at the bottom. Knickers or plus fours were big with sportsmen and were buckled four inches below the knee, hence the name 'plus fours'.

Lighter colors were favored in summer but cold weather called for another of those items which makes an age memorable — the raccoon coat. All the college boys had them an some of the co-eds too. I inherited a raccoon coat in perfect condition and wore it in the 1950's. Recently I saw a young man in San Francisco sporting just such a coat. It was like a one man fashion show. The raccoon coat, a great coat in every sense of the word, useful, stylish even now, and large, larger even than life.

That was the 1920's . . .

If the 1920's prove one half of the adage that hemlines go up when the stock market goes up, the 1930's surely prove the other half, the hemlines go down when the stock market drops. By 1930 skirts were longer, and the waistline was again in its normal place, nothing else seemed normal though.

When historians refer to the 30's, we read about "the great depression", the songwriters were asking, "Brother can you Spare a Dime", but fashion dictators were advising longer hair, wider shoulders, narrow hips and in evening new emphasis on the back.

Many Americans can recall the time with great clarity. As children, the depression shaped their futures in all ways, and encouraged a sense of caution. Many, left with a sense of thrift born in those difficult days, never discarded the clothing of that period and so collectors today have an opportunity not always possible when dealing with other times; except for Art Deco fans, not too many collectors have taken advantage of the opportunity.

For years clothing of the period was neglected. People who had lived through the bleak years did not want to be reminded and the young had not yet begun to consider the rather shapeless day wear attractive. But as we continue to be more removed in time from the 30's we can focus on what was good rather than bad and can decide what a good collection should include.

The best of the clothing and the evening wear is only now attracting buyers in numbers. At no time, for example, has there been a more simple but classic design than the plain black velvet evening dress of the 30's. It is so characteristic that collectors simply refer to it as "the thirties black velvet". It is stark and beautiful, can be worn unadorned or with ornamentation equally well. That, in fact, may be a summation of the 30's fashion scene.

America's dress image became blurred — factories were manufacturing clothing by the ton — and anybody who could afford it could wear any clothes that appealed. This was the early period of homogenization and where once clothing defined social status and the role in life, now the rich continued to patronize the great design houses, the college students wanted to look like workers and began to adopt the Levis, and clothing no longer labeled the wearer.

Clothing was made for every conceivable use and wardrobes

began expanding. There was a very wide range of fashions. Sportwear was a big item at this time, tennis was fashionable, but skating was geared more toward the average person and the costumes are pretty and available. In most of the feminine apparel at this time, in sportswear as well, the waistline was natural and bosoms were accentuated.

The 1930's brought dramatic changes to the fashion picture. The zipper came into wide use and it takes little imagination to realize what its convenience meant, and in 1939 — nylon. The zipper replaced all those buttons or other closures and nylon revolutionized the clothing industry.

Other surprising things came out of the thirties, Hollywood coined some memorable words — 'glamour' was one. It's hard to imagine how we ever lived without the word and harder still to realize it was part of the depression years.

Another faint shock can be felt when reading the women's magazines of 1930. They were devoting many pages to fashion. Perhaps as an antidote to the times. Ski clothes, if you can visualize that, were being touted, "winter sports are becoming more important each year and comfort is the first requisite. Smart women," they said, "are forsaking modernistic designs in favor of somber colors, such as black, navy or brown, the long trouser suits in serge or gabardine or waterproof whipcord with brightly colored accessories, and a heavy woolen shirt should be tucked into the trousers that fit tightly over the hips." It was a somewhat classic look, and while certainly not in tune with the ski clothes of today, could be worn without seeming out of place.

Another publication was promoting "Fashions for the South". These were beach attire which was becoming quite racy, backless, large armholes, no overskirts, with a deep decolletage. Also the one piece tennis dresses, casual lightweight jackets and the long, straight evening wear.

The clothing collector is perfectly justified in seeking out these garments which were worn, for the most part, by people of means, who bought the best and took care of it. The average person wore garments until necessity decreed a replacement and while these are often very easily found, it is a problem to get them in mint condition.

The House of Worth was showing "restaurant" or informal evening wear with low decolletage and low back edged with a band of green and white beads. The materials could be very rich, Worth used brocades and chiffons and velvets. While not everyone can own a Worth, the evening wear of the thirties is what many collectors are seeking. I have recently seen several gowns in excellent condition and prices on clothes of this type have only begun a rather steep rise.

Practical, though, was the word for most day wear. Belts were popular around the normal waistline, skirts flared from the knee down, touches of white at the neck was considered a nice touch. Often you will see these little collars thrown in boxes of unknowing antique shop dealers and you should be alert to what they are.

Wool crepe, which wore well, was used for daytime clothes and velvet predominated at night. The jabot, which was a cascade of frills down the front of the dress or shirt, was high style.

Although collectors have somewhat neglected the 1930's, it was actually a time when fashion had much to commend it. The clothes were fairly simple and practical; bows at the chin, or on one shoulder, or attached low on one hip were a flattering device; the quality was excellent, both as to fabric and finish and they were comfortable. The beret, the cloche, and the 'large, garden-party' hats vied with soft felt, flat straw and the turban.

In our mind's eye, we consider the fashions of the 1930's somewhat dowdy. To those who remember the housedress, a plain, utilitarian garment if ever there was one, but oh, so comfortable and useful, or the everyday dresses of the less affluent, this is understandable, but the better clothing, well made and well designed, hung gracefully on the figure and in truth was a flattering style. Worn with the tightly fitting hats or turbans and overlaid with fascinating furs, it could be alluring. It was a style particularly suited to the person with an ingrained sense of elegance and yes, flair. It was essentially a streamlined fashion and much of it is mistaken for clothing of the 20's.

The cloche hats are almost impossible to tell apart, the strap shoes were worn into the thirites, the dresses themselves are often labeled incorrectly and this is where knowledge of waistlines and necklines can be important. This is why, too, anyone who is collecting should try to get any possible information from the dealer and why anyone who is scouring trunks and attics should get the family history.

It is indeed difficult for almost anyone to differentiate clothing made during transitional periods. The styles of the 1928-29 period were already showing the flared skirt, but were shorter, waistlines had risen by 1928-29 but were still lower than those found on the 30's clothes. It becomes increasingly important to the collector to know exactly what the collecting goal is. A lovely, general collection of old clothes, a certain kind of clothing, regardless of period, or, as is always advisable, the clothing of a given time segment. Buy what appeals and is affordable and fit your collection within an overall category of years. Buy what is typical of the period and do not worry overmuch whether the garment or hat was made in 1929 or 1931.

Mail order which really caught on in the 1920's was big business in the 30's and ready-made clothes prospered along with the catalogues. The first fashion illustration ever to appear in such a catalogue was published by Montgomery Ward in 1878. These old catalogues, many in reprint, are wonderful source materials for the collector. When I peruse these, I feel transported back in time and get the urge to pick up the phone and order what I see displayed.

Some of the favorite features of 1930's clothing are still popular, the jabot, the scarf collar which could be tied anyway you pleased, and the lovely deep fur trimmed coats which had the collar set back from the face and yet framed it.

These coats in good condition are bargains at any reasonable price. Well made and beautifully furred and usually wool, they oftentimes cost less than a gown or suit and are lovely to look at, or wear.

If there was one typical daytime style of the 30's it was the print dress. As yet, there are not too many of these available but they should be searched out. Women really loved these bright, cheerful prints, either in small closely spaced figures or medium sized, widely spaced. They often had cape effects or jackets, and for hot weather they were adapted to lighter materials and made sleeveless. This passion for print was one of the characteristics of this time.

Shoes were pumps with bows, or the plain walking pump, or the leather oxford, or the one strap. Kid was the most chosen material, but calf and patent leather were also in favor. Pumps were the favorites, but the reptile skinned shoes made an impact which carried over to later years. The toe could be elongated or pointed and a very attractive type for collectors were the evening shoes with buckle trim, the buckle was part of the shoe itself.

The notable shoe from the 30's was worn for sports activities. It was an oxford with the fringed, outside tongue. This covered the laces and is another of those immediately recognizable styles that can be dated at a glance. Interestingly enough, men's clothing is so scarce that in searching for a collection of men's clothing on any large scale, particularly a comprehensive shoe collection, I sought but did not find.

It was in the 30's that the idea of promoting sales of men's clothing could be based on snob appeal was advanced. Clothing designers and manufacturers have always known that if enough changes are made in garments to render them out of fashion in a short time, more sales will be made as women would rush out to refurbish but this concept had not been widely applied to men's clothes. It was also the time that men began to discard undershirts, supposedly because movie star Clark Gable took off his shirt and only bare chest was visible. Warm shirts in large plaids, and early in the decade the single breasted jacket was the male look. Later, jackets became double breasted and the front of the jacket was higher.

One of the radical changes in women's wear in America during the 30's was the latex girdle. It was flexible and moved with the body and became enormously popular. It was a far cry from the whalebone corset. It was lightweight and could be easily laundered. Even in those days there were obviously some fashion rebels for recently I happened upon several of these girdles unworn, but unfortunately not boxed.

"Never were boxed," said the owner, they were bought off store counters and I never wore a girdle at all." These are interesting and if in pristine condition when found, should not yet cost much.

Another drastic change was the neckline. The halter neckline was introduced and caught on. This neckline has survived and prospered, and as with many earlier styles is now being revived by designers and shown on new clothing.

In the late 30's and early 40's traditional modesty was challenged with the introduction of the bare midriff. As with all clever clothing, it was simply an indication of things to come. Fashion always seems to anticipate events.

As net and lacy trifles began to replace hats, the industry quaked. The automobile contributed to the trend, a closed car required no head cover. The hat began to fade as a prime requisite of dress and the industry was further crushed when the Catholic Church announced that the feminine head no longer needed to be covered in church. The hat has all but disappeared except for utilitarian purposes, making the hats of the thirties fine collectibles. Almost the last hurrah of a fashion survivor.

The jewelry of the thirties should be considered just that and has already found a huge market. However, there are certain pieces, such as the dress clips, the belt buckles and the shoe clips of the late 30's which should be added to a clothing collection. The pairs of clips which attached to a dress neckline are particularly desirable. Often this type jewelry is chunky art deco rather than the rare platinum and diamond pieces from the same era. The everyday decorations that women wore have an appeal that is not easily defined, but appeal it does.

Schiaparelli was a product of the thirties and her chief contribution was color — shocking pink became a rage. She had a sense of fun and many of the things she designed seemed outrageous, but she influenced fashion and a Schiaparelli label is something to boast of in a collection. There is a whole new collecting area, not the clothing collector, but the collector of labels in the clothing.

It makes for a surprisingly beautiful collection, the labels are varying sizes and while the new ones are mostly machine woven the older ones are so lovely that the backs resemble needlepoint. The woven ones are much harder to find than they were a year or two ago, the owner of a large collection tells me and "most of them on cheaper clothing are stamped now." If this kind of collection catches on, and already I know of several fine collections, what will happen to the designer-identified gown?

Long beads were still worn at the end of the decade, but chokers lived happily with the V-neckline. The beret was a fitting companion to the slim fitting jackets of the suits, but it was but one of many of the diverse hat styles. America itself was diverse and diversifying, but soon had its course decided for it.

The 1930's were years of depression, then of hope, and finally of war. A stirring ten years, but regardless of other happenings the thirties proves that the influence of fashion goes on.

A particularly graceful chiffon beaded dress with large bow. 1923. Value $500-550.

Short, beaded evening dress, 1927, beautifully designed, $550-650. Feather boa, $85-95. Photo by Kenn Knackstedt. Courtesy Southern Oregon Historical Society.

1924. All dresses of this year fall into the $125-175 range, unless beaded or unusually designed and decorated.

Dresses: left, $45-60; right, $130-150.

Dresses: $50-60 value range.

Dresses: $50-60 value range.

1927 tea frock. V-neck and cape sleeves. Skirt falls far below the knee. Made from contemporary pattern. Value of original $55-65. Courtesy of Folkwear, San Rafael, Ca.

1935. Cape effects were widely used in 1935-1936 and 1937. Dresses of this type as shown in this 1935 advertisement were designed for the woman who was "36 or more", on up to size 50. Dresses of this type range $50-60 if short, long gowns range $125-150. Dresses of this era are beginning to be avidly sought after.

1930's black velvet dress. Unadorned except for slits in material at back of neckline. This is a genuine clothing classic. $325-375.

C. 1935-1938. Bias cut evening dress with rhinestone studding, white crepe, V-neck with low, open back. Value $195-225.

Blouses have wide price variations. This type, $45-55. 2
piece skirt, $95-100. Negligee, $125-150.

1920's satin beaded dress. Two piece, large size, skirt lined. Extremely heavy. Value, $500-550.

Black satin and pink chiffon 1920's beaded dress. Beading on front attached panel only. Value $375-425.

1939 two piece skating outfit. Both jacket and skirt reversible, red velvet one side, plaid the other, double breasted with hood. Value $150-190.

Striped beaver coat of the 1930's. Front and rear view to show striping. $900-1,000.

Ocelot jacket, 1939, $650-750.

Monkey coat, 1939-1940. Silk lining, corde collar. Value $1,500-1,750.

Early 1920's grey-blue silk velvet coat with chinchilla trim. Silk crepe lining. Weighted in hem. Value $1,750-2,000.

One piece under-garment, pink silk, lace insets and trim. Satin ribbons. c. 1930. Value $95-120.

1930's 'Satin Dasche' panties, buttoned on side. Darker lace trim. $32-37.

150

Child's French satin bed garment. Lace and satin, rosette at neckline. Made in Paris. Value $100-115.

Lounging pajamas, 1920's, 50 percent silk, 50 percent rayon, machine made lace sewn onto pajamas. Value $95-125.

Underthings of 1924: Camisole tops: silk, $95-110; cotton, $55-65. Corsets of this period: $40-45. Combinations (bottom row) $45-50, these are characteristics of the 20's silhouette.

153

1930's hats: top $25-30; center $25-30; bottom, $28-32.

Accessories, 1920's, 1930's. Left to right: hat stand, top covered in velvet with rhinestones, c. 1920, value $30-35. Hat form, painted with bobbed hair, c. 1928, $35-45. Rhinestone necklace, hand set stones, $42-50. Rhinestone bag, chain handles, c. 1930's, $75-80. Garters, 1920's each $22-27. Satin shoes, ankle straps, buttons, c. 1929, $70-80. Cigarette holder, $32-38.

1928 hats, $125-150.

1925. Hats of the 20's and of this type have a range of $125-150, but prices are rising.

The striking hats of the 20's are always desirable to collectors. If hats are of this beauty and quality the range should be $125-150.

Men's straw boaters, 1920's except for top which is 1940's. Bottom right is unusual weave. Values, $30-40.

1931. Long scarf, $25-27. Shorties scarves and ties, $20-25.

"Silver foxes" worn over 30's velvet dress. Net and velvet bow headpiece, c. 1936-37. Fur piece, $300-350. Net 'hat'. This has no frame so is considered a veil. $20-25.

1924. Beads were so popular that women wore beads on beads. Long 20's glass beads, value $45-55. Men's 20's tuxedoes, value $175-185.

1930's shoes (unworn), $50-60.

162

Fancy apron, 1930's, hand embroidered, $35-50.

Children's wear, 1924, top row: $20-25, $22-27; $22-27; $35-40 Bottom: $20-25.

164

Children's wear, 1924, left: $30-35, $20-25.

Children's wear, 1924, right: $38-48, $30-35.

Girls' wear, 1924. Dresses, $35-40.
Coat, $40-45.

Young girl's party dress, worn by 7 year old in 1930. Gorgette and lace. Value $90-120.

Light blue rayon jacquard trimmed with lace. Child's christening coat, worn around 1925. Value $85-110.

1936. Young girl's party dress. Taffeta with attached belt. Value $125-145.

CHAPTER IV
1940 - 1960

In 1939, there was no reason to suppose that fashion would go into hiding. United States involvement in the war took us all by surprise, but its reality forced much of the fashion industry to sit it out. So many people can remember the 40's, they lived through those years and many have told me that reading about fashion is not like living with fashion. The average person wore what was appropriate, what had been dictated by some designer and made available.

In general the rather static state of fashion in the early 1940's stemmed from uncertainty and a sense of the fitness of things, drastic changes would have seemed unpatriotic. "From now until the war is won, we won't have radical changes in fashion" was the fashion decree.

Waste of anything, including material, was to be avoided, and the Government asked the designers not to use unnecessary lengths of fabric, not make extreme changes, not to use excessive trimmings, in short, let the silhouette alone. One of the results of this dictum was cuffless slacks, and patterns of that date proudly stated the limited material it would take to make such and such a garment.

The lack of new directions for clothes did not quench the everlasting feminine search for chic. John Whitcomb, the talented illustrator (whose work is now being collected) delineated the 40's female in the ideaized way the Gibson Girl spoke for the Nineties. In time this fascinating female he depicted will become the nostalgia buff's pin-up.

It was a time when evening wear was seductive, and day wear had a neat simplicity. The dirndl skirt went well with a shirtwaist top, and the jacketed suit dress could go anywhere comfortably. Necklines were varied, choices were many, but the plunging neckline was a favorite.

Joan Crawford's squared shoulders speak for the time. This padded, wide shoulder was typical, but there were dresses with soft folds which fell gracefully, the black dress might have white lace edging on the revers and short sleeves, and the 'dickey' was considered "a high spot" of many frocks. It was worn under the dress so it presented a collar on a collar usually in contrasting colors. Anybody who ever owned or wore a 'dickey' can tell you it was one of the handiest things ever designed.

"The suit dress is the civilian's uniform for summer," said a popular magazine. It could be severely tailored or made in softer materials and draped, but the shoulders were padded and square. Saddle stitching was part of many dresses and the princess line was evident in the early 40's. The shirtwaist dress was given a new twist — "something different in the 'shirtfrock' were the suspender like tucks, with the curved pockets following the line of the saddle stitching.

There were luscious colors in dresses and dress suits, and there were still some prints.

As with most coats, there seem to be few collectors. The boxy coat of the 40's was padded at the shoulders and could be had in almost any length from waist to hem. The classic town coat was sometimes called a 'reefer' and was a fitted and flattering style. The technique of using long, narrow panels to make it, slenderized the figure. There are many still around, and being rapidly pulled out of closets.

It may very well be the square shoulders that attracts, but whatever the reason it is toward the 40's that today's younger collectors are aiming. From the vantage point of those who wore them some of the exaggerated styles of the 40's do not seem that long ago, to those who were born in the 1960's they have such a different look as to be almost 'camp'.

Everywhere the vintage clothing stores are catering to this younger trade, some of whom are buying to wear, some to collect. The early 40's costumes were military oriented — in feminine attire this was reflected in the wide-shouldered, nipped-in waist look.

In men's clothing gabardine and khaki were being worn and colors were rather muted in keeping with the times. The military uniforms were seen everywhere, and now they are a big segment of clothing collecting. There are military shops devoted to the sale of these as well as anything connected with any of our branches of service. A lighter touch during this period was the porkpie hat, which was well liked for its flat crown and snap brim, it proved to be an enduring fashion.

Slacks, which had become necessary in the factories, were gaining favor, but slowly. It was a time of Rosie the Riveter and as she riveted, she needed suitable clothing. Although, we in the United States, are hard put to remember the pre-jeans era, this was it. When slacks did start to become part of the wardrobe, they were utilitarian and comfortable, they were, in fact, a bit on the baggy side, but they opened the way for the jeans revolution. In 1949 there were 'dungarees' or 'western style pants'. No one could ever have foreseen the effect these pants would have on future fashion, if they had, probably every design house would have dropped everything and geared up for production. Now we have high fashion jeans and poor Levi Strauss must be twirling in his grave, at the sexy image.

It was the young Christian Dior who created consternation with his New Look in 1947. It was introduced in Paris and was not an immediate sensation. It was distinctly feminine in feeling, a rounded look, and Dior dropped the hemline with a thud heard round the world. The shoulder was rounded and the small waistline emphasized. The fashion permeated every segment of society and the tiny flowered hats sporting veils, or the veils on frames, are now eagerly sought after. They are very flattering, are well made, and many have survived. Hat

171

collectors adore them, they take less space than older hats and come in a wide variety. They can still be worn with confidence, since they coordinate well with almost any costume, and are still inexpensive.

This was the time of matching the color of the gloves with the outfit, and if ever there is an underrated collecting field it is gloves. Fortunately the gloves of the 40's seem to have spurred many young people to buy them and care for them and I know of several good collections. It's amazing how few collectors look for them. They are often in beautiful shades of colors, and may have embroidery, or have the hand-tied French knots. The soft kid gloves of the 40's are especially fine, but prices on these have made substantial gains, possibly because people are impressed with the 'Made in France' label many of them carry. The gauntlet type have a distinctive look and the wrist length, or the long evening gloves with the little pearl buttons have often sold to those interested in jewelry or buttons. I wonder how many gloves have been sacrificed this way?

The dedicated clothing collector should keep in mind that while the great designers were providing fashion to the wealthy, America's off-the-rack capability was the finest in the world. Indeed it was not until the very late 1950's that Europe tried this way of merchandising, so most of the clothing available to us was probably bought off-the-rack and does not bear the great designer labels. If one were to find dresses with a Hattie Carnegie or Adrian label it would be a tremendous acquisition, but excellent copies, or New York's 7th Avenue originals are what we are most apt to add to our collections. Haute Couture boasts intricate and clever tailoring which flatters the figure and thus can command astronomical prices, but surely part of the price is paying for the label. Still, Paris was calling the tune.

When Dior decreed skirts should rise only 12 or 15 inches off the ground, women everywhere responded and discarded whole wardrobes in order to conform. The new dress code required high heels so the shoe image changed from the clunky, somewhat awkward footwear of the earlier 40's to the slimmer heel. This is an interesting period in shoes, the toes being round but blunted. It is difficult to visualize a collection of shoes, but having viewed one, properly set out, is to become a convert.

The really wonderful aspect of Dior and his 'New Look' is that we do not have to wade through transitional clothing, the whole world knows, almost precisely to the minute, when Dior announced his new style. This circumstance is unique to clothing collectors and we should be properly grateful. We also know exactly when the fashion ended, by 1949 the style was phasing out and hemlines rose and the silhouette became less flaring. We who collect, or deal in clothing, can thank Dior for making the 1940's so exciting for us.

Seeking the couturier clothing involves some canny planning. Often the best source is the thrift shops maintained by women's auxiliaries whose members claim some social standing. If their social life is busy and requires much formal wear, they will often donate their outdated wardrobes to the thrift shops to which they volunteer. Recently, such a shop, a tiny one, in Westchester County, New York, boasted dresses by Norell and Mary Quant, and labels such as Saks, 5th Avenue, Marshall Field and Lilli Ann. These were all day dresses, all of 40's and 50's vintage, and all together would have cost less than $50. Each of them a great addition to any collection.

The truth is that superior tailoring does not easily become dated, and often you will find women wearing couturier clothing made years ago. It is largely a revolutionary style, such as the 'New Look' which demands an entirely new wardrobe to keep in fashion. Nowadays we tend to ignore such a dictum from the arbiters of fashion and independence in dress is following independence in action.

So it is wise to track down shops run by organizations such as the Junior League, famous hospital auxiliaries and annual benefit auctions and sales put on by groups of socialites to benefit some worthy cause. These annual affairs, which sometimes benefit museums and branches of the arts, are probably some of the more serious places to shop for vintage, high-fashion clothing.

To do this, the collector has to read the newspapers diligently to keep aware of the upcoming sales. Some organizations will put you on their mailing list for occasions of this kind and if it is possible, request this. Usually clothing at these sales cost very little, since they are essentially high class rummage sales, and you will no doubt find many good buys. It does take time and effort but this can be rewarding.

Resale Shops are often the source of good finds, but tend to be more expensive since they must buy and clean clothing and do any repairing, and must also maintain a good looking shop in order to attract customers.

Goodwill, Salvation Army and St. Vincent de Paul were once treasure troves of older clothing, but their donations are off and competition among collectors who frequent these places is much keener. There are many people who know the exact time of donated merchandise deliveries and manage in that way to secure the goodies. Recently, though, a local St. Vincent de Paul had a remarkable collection of vintage shoes with buckles and bows which were being sold for $5 each pair, and were intended for wear with costumes on Halloween. Goodwill saves some of its better donated vintage clothing for its annual fashion show put on by the Goodwill Bags, but take a look if you're passing, because vintage clothing, like any other antique, is where you find it. But in this field today, you certainly have to keep looking.

Shoe collectors have a more difficult task since shoes have often been discarded as wear and tear make them less acceptable to good dress. There are rising numbers of people who are looking for vintage shoes. Reduced availability and sometimes less than perfect condition makes the search for old shoes discouraging to the faint hearted. The find, though, is well worth the hunt. Shoes of the 1940's are wholly unique. They can be clumsy looking and in no way resemble the footwear of the 1920's or earlier periods. Studious collectors should note that footwear can be categorized by the way the sole is attached to the upper.

American Footwear Industry lists 'cemented' when the sole and heel are attached by adhesion; 'molded' when the sole and heel are formed and the attachment to the upper is accomplished within a mold; 'sewn' is when the sole is attached to the upper by a stitched seam. The old method of nailing sole to upper was considered obsolete, which is a good time judgment for collectors.

Shoe styles have evolved and changed, often quite drastically, and are among the very typical artifacts of a given era. The wedgies of the 40's, the fairly narrow open toes, the tie oxford, are all characteristic.

The bulky look shoe complemented the dirndl dress and the military looking suit was perfect with the oxford. The 'peep toes' were the dress shoe of the day. As a 'go with' to shoe collecting the old wooden shoe forms are ideal. In this area though you compete with the antique collector and the interior decorator, take heart, they can't be everywhere.

With the end of World War II came a lighter look, and the mink stole was worn everywhere except the supermarket. The ubiquitous mink stole of that period has not made the comeback that other vintage furs, such as the silver fox jacket and neckpiece have achieved, but considering the small prices at which these stoles are marked, they are an excellent investment.

The 40's from beginning to end were a special time in America. The red, white and blue color scheme was used in clothing, there were ration cards, nylon hose, when available, was a cause of long lines, the hats are collectible but when worn today are not tilted over the eyebrow as was de rigeur in the 40's, but at a more flattering angle further back on the head.

The 40's was turban time. A classic fashion which has appeared and reappeared in some form, the turban was in part an answer to the demands of safety, to keep hair out of machinery at which women now worked in numbers. They affected snoods and hair nets and they started the passion for pants.

As the 1940's began, fashion direction was uncertain, but people in general were becoming much more casual about dress. This decade really marked the beginning of informality and complete independence from rigid fashion demands.

As the decade ended it became memorable for synthetic fibers, the boxy, square shoulders and the return of the female figure, for boleros and the "New Look". For clothing collectors the indicators of

40's fashions are the smaller hat, the square, padded shoulders, narrow waist. The strapless evening gown, supposedly held up by a prayer, was almost standard. The military influence lent itself to the Eisenhower jacket both for men and women, and pea coats and khaki sportswear remained popular for men.

The years 1940 to 1950 are one of the strongest in the clothing collecting field. Several years ago it began to attract young people, both male and female, and the trend continues. No wonder, it seems to have everything a good collection demands, unique styling, short skirts, long skirts, strapless gowns, luxurious furs, coats of many designs, unusual shoes, and lovely handbags. There is very little the collector cannot find from the 40's, to fit his purse and preference. Close your eyes, make a clothing wish, then check out the 1940's.

As the country moved into a new decade we seemed to be searching for security. Conservatism was the new creed. This is especially reflected in the menswear of the early 1950's when the trim, quiet look was in vogue. This was a distinct change from the late 1940's brighter colors. Now dark shades of blue and brown and gray took over the scene. In 1953 the gray flannel suit began its reign.

President Eisenhower refused to bow to tradition at his inauguration in 1953 when he chose to wear a jacket with his striped trousers and a homburg instead of the usual top hat and cutaway. Looking back on his decision, it seems merely the choice of a man who wanted more informality, a less rigid way of dealing with ordinary affairs. In reality, it was a ripple on the surface of what was to become almost a full scale revolt by the young. It was a forerunner of entirely new directions both in clothing and lifestyle, and Elvis Presley was waiting in the wings with his levis and suede shoes.

The second World War emancipated everyone, and fashion was on the way to becoming anything anyone wanted it to be. If the early 50's had any typical characteristics it was probably the normal waistline, narrow slim skirts at mid-calf which were soon to shorten again. The A line which Dior ordained in 1958 had a very wide skirt draped from sloping shoulders, and the skirt just below the knee. As the 50's progressed so did the skirt, upward.

This was generally a period of transition when almost anything was acceptable. Some of the full skirts of the 40's persisted into the early fifties. The long fitted bodice of 1954 and 1955 emphasized a beautiful figure. The focus was on the neckline and hipline, and dresses were usually worn with the pointed shoe with high slender heels. Heels on the shoes became even higher before the end of the decade. They were considered a menace and were decried by promoters of good posture.

The bustline was accentuated, the waistline was high, and the strapless evening gown was still being worn by the end of 1958. Knitwear, especially the Chanel style jacketed dress and suit became classic and went easily from office to cocktails. The pillbox hat was sitting pertly on most female heads, but with the modified cloche hats, organza veilings, very tiny hats, wide brimmed hats, headbands, small feather confections, the hat collector can have a field day with the 50's.

Recently, while I was browsing in a small vintage clothing shop, an elderly lady approached me in a state of high excitement. "Look at this," she exclaimed, holding up a rather nondescript gray straw hat, "this is a Dior, look at the label." I did. It surely was a Dior, if rather faded, and since she explained she was a hat collector I could understand her exuberance. The label itself was large and striking, it was a vintage hat, and the price was not very high, and no doubt she felt she had a bargain. I would have recommended perhaps, a hat bearing no label, which sat on a nearby stand and was of the same vintage — a small, crescent shape with a mesh veil, flowers on the crown and a velvet ribbon flat bow, an enticing affair and costing just a bit less. There was that label, though, and we collectors have to make our choices. Vintage clothing bearing designer labels will usually cost more. "Snob appeal", one dealer says.

This is not true for shoe collectors, the label does not make the shoe, except for a few outstanding makers and the mark of an exclusive shoe store. Most dealers price according to condition and era. Collectors who buy also to wear are concerned with fit, and this is a frustrating situation. The 50's shoes are fairly easy to find, although here again, their appeal to younger collectors causes the fine examples to sell quickly. These very high, slender heels are more difficult to find, the styles without sides or cut deeply on the sides are very flattering to the foot, but the smallish, open toes are the big goal. The alligator and lizard skin shoes and handbags of this era are intrinsically valuable but condition should be good. Many closets still harbor shoes of this period.

Budget conscious collectors should visit their thrift shops more often. In a recent tour I found large numbers of the 50's coats. These were unusually attractive, especially in the late 50's. Dior (the man did everything) had introduced his A line with its wide hemline and narrow shoulders and these are found frequently. The tie neckline also is a very pretty style. There are also the very typical three quarter length coats and the shortie coats with the belt in the back. Another attractive coat from that period has the shawl collar and narrow hem which is often furred. People who buy and wear these coats profess to admire their 'old fashioned' look. People who buy then as a collectible have found a veritable gold mine.

The sheath was the big news in the 50's and in keeping with the times it was an easy and comfortable style. Women were seen everywhere in this narrow but unconfining dress. Capri pants and the skirts — circle skirts, were wide and often stiffened. The total ensemble was usually skirt and blouse or capri pants, or skirt with sweater or blouse. Handbags were casual and that was the attraction of the shoulder bag.

Handbags are a joy to collect. Not as pretty as the beaded bags or as intricately worked as the tapestries, not as spectacular as the best of the art deco, the 50's handbags have a special place. They often have unusual handles of metal, leather or plastic. Reptile skin was commonly used and some women were still carrying the corde.

As always with pocketbooks or purses, shapes are quite varied, and it is often the handles that lend interest. It is almost a cliche to say that fashion comes full circle every generation, but there is ample proof that this is true. Several times recently I have used a heavy leather shoulder bag from the 50's. It is finely made and has a heavy gilt closure. It is large enough to hold all the necessities and it still strikes a fashion note. There is a timelessness about some things and good leather, simply worked, is one. Except for the wide, braided shoulder strap which was used frequently on bags of this type in the 50's, only the most sophisticated fashion critic could date the bag.

Gifts for the men in the years of the early 50's included a Shaefer 'snorkel fountain pen', which would be a great find; or a yellow and black striped Italian denim butler's jacket, which would be useful if you wanted to impress guests; and waterproof deerskin slippers with foam rubber lining, at $12.50 a pair.

Ski parkas were being touted in bright colors and 'warmly lined for warmth'.

Clear plastic umbrellas cheered the rainy days, and a wool jersey scarf lined in hand printed silk was the offering from 'Vera'. Today a complete and very thorough collection of scarves by 'Vera' could easily be made, they seem to turn up everywhere.

Mother and Daughter dresses were popular. A charming collection this would be — the adult's dress and the matching child's dress displayed side by side. Almost like collecting in pairs, the large and the miniature. To date, I have found only two such pairs and they are in a private collection. Should a person happen on a set and the dealer would be foolish enough to break it up, don't hesitate, buy both. Not only were they eye-catching in their day, and interesting to us today, but think of the future and how unusual the matching pieces will be.

Hats of both mother and daughter often matched too, but it is almost too much to expect that 4 such articles will be found intact. Still, it's intriguing and cries out for a determined collector. Someone with an eye for the unusual. It is these fads which sustain popularity for awhile and then disappear which sometimes become the basis for the most valuable collections.

Plisse was an oft-heard name in the early 50's, but we don't hear it too much anymore. It is cotton, with a crinkle effect and usually patterned. It was 'easy iron' and was widely used in nightwear and

177

some of the nightgowns from which it was made, are attractive enough to be worn for summer evening wear. Many plisse garments are striped or have small prints and almost all are very pretty. When some young collector decides this is the case, you may see a brightly colored plisse printed nightgown of the 1950's doing double duty.

With the variety of fabrics available in the 1950's, it is probably safe to say that lingerie could be made of almost any material. It is also safe to say that it was exceedingly lovely for the most part. The shortie nightie which ended just below the knee sometimes had tiny sleeves or cape effects and touches of lace and ribbon which made for a dainty, delightful morsel. The colors, petal pink, or heaven blue, or even buttercup are delectable. Longer gowns were also worn, many of them made of nylon tricot which boasted the same 'easy care'. Nylon is a high-strength, resilient synthetic, so many survive today. This is a great time to collect these pretty things including the full underslips and the handy half slips which have wide lace trim.

Barbizon was the big name in lingerie if you are label conscious, but there were many manufacturers producing beautiful underwear. Some of the fancy slips are made in the gored fashion which prevented bunching at the waist. They were expertly tailored and make a wonderful collection. It was one of the best of times for women's undergarments and before these get away from us we should make every effort to include them in our collections. They require little care and make a colorful display.

The undergarments fitted well under the clothing. One of the most delightful of fashions in the 50's was the 2 piece suit, jacket and skirt, in rayon gabardine. The jacket was short, with a flare and a Peter Pan collar with double rows of buttons, the skirt was straight and fairly narrow. It was one of those outfits which went everywhere, and I have seen several similar outfits lately, so it must have been a big seller. It was practical, maybe that's why. Women were losing their zest for using a different garment for every occasion and a dress that went through the day was a plus. With this 2 piece suit the whole look could be changed with a new sweater or blouse and with the jacket left open.

Dolman sleeves were still being worn in the 50's and the loose, and longish sweater often had them. The Dolman sleeve is one of the most comfortable ever devised, so it's easy to see that we had moved even deeper into our desire for ease and practicality in clothes.

The Italian fashion collections became very important and without doubt they had a flair for color and design which began to take the lead in certain directions. They introduced innovative ski wear and magnificent shoe styles. It wasn't the Italians, though, who created a sensation in the tennis world. It was Ted Tinling who dressed Gussie Moran in lace trimmed panties which caused a furor. She played at Wimbledon in 1949, and those panties banished forever the image of the staid and proper tennis buff.

A small development really, that Moran outfit, completely modest by today's standards, but it led to a new fashion standard for tennis players and more enjoyment for fans. One reporter maintained that people were going to watch tennis when Gussie played only to see what she would wear.

Tennis gear is collectible on all levels, the tennis wear itself is an excellent collectible because it did not change much until 1949. Since that time it has become as varied as one could want. The dresses were usually white, one piece and belted and pleated. By the 40's the one piece dress was shorter, and soon the outfit became two pieces. Tennis dresses are distinctive and to a sportsminded person would present an exciting challenge. I do not know anyone with such a collection so it has a relatively open future. As with anything that has not yet really caught on, prices should be minimal.

Many things from the 50's are ideal collectibles. The eyeglasses are strictly for fun and profit. Rhinestones or brilliants were set into plastic frames which were called 'harlequin' and looked like a giant butterfly. Until about a year ago, these could be bought for a dollar or two anywhere, now they are commanding prices of $5-25 depending on their amount of decoration and how bizarre they are. Women are wearing them and there is a trend to buy a pair and replace the lenses with you own prescription. They are certainly conversation pieces. These wild spectacles did not much influence men's eye wear, they were still sporting the horn rims.

There is much to commend the 1950's as a collecting field, but for many it is still too close.

Designers appreciate it and many adaptions of the 40's and 50's styles are evident in the new clothing.

The 1950's are a closed chapter which many of us remember vividly, and that makes it easy to dismiss the 50's as yet too recent to be considered vintage fashion. The collecting world has become so competitive and unpredictable that it is almost dangerous to discard anything made yesterday.

On that note, the 1950's seem akin to the dinosaur age. Much of the clothing has not yet come out of the closet, and thrifty women everywhere have saved a quantity of it, now hanging neatly all in a row and never worn. Yet they cannot part with it.

When more of it comes into the marketplace, potential collectors will be surprised at its beauty, its charm or its whimsy, depending on the mood.

Collecting is largely a point of view. From the vantage point of 1983, it may be difficult to keep the 1950's in perspective. Try — the fashions of those years may bring big rewards.

1960

A peek into the 1960's should send collectors scurrying about to try to amass a collection of that decade's most controversial style — the mini skirt. It looked great on young, long-stemmed American beauties, on all others it was an abomination.

Mary Quant evoked it, and has been quoted recently as saying that she felt at the time that the 1960's needed "a revolution" and frankly admits that it was intended as a fashion for the young. In fact, it seems to have been an acknowledgement that young people were a major market, they had plenty of money to spend and were more than willing to spend it.

There were other styles and other happenings during the following years, there are other clothes and other accessories to search for, but at this time, before they disappear, the collector should be alert to the mini.

Fifty years from now the uninitiated are going to look at all those minis and think, Gosh, people were short in the 1960's.

1940's dress. Black crepe with peplum and sleeves trimmed in sequins. Accessories include black cotton cut-worked embroidered gloves, sequined hat with feather, snood and a stole of four stone martins. Values: dress, $110-120; fur piece, $200-225; gloves, $15-20; hat, $20-35.

Two piece outfit from the 1940's. Quilted blue midi length skirt worn with Lilli Ann of San Francisco jacket, dark blue textured wool accented with white bead work on collar and on the wide cuffed sleeves. Skirt, value $45-70. Jacket, value $45-55. Model is wearing a snood.

Blue cotton lace with attached taffeta underslip. Cocktail or 'mother-of-the-Bride' dress. 1952. Tasteful, small rhinestone patterns on collar. Value, $150-160. Blue gray kid shoes, worn with dress originally. Value $40-50.

Blue ruffled chiffon over taffeta underskirt. Worn in 1941. Value, $95-125.

Two piece jacket dress, self cuffs, raglan sleeves, sateen. C. 1944. Value, $95-110.

1944. Blue wool coat, fitted, white fox collar, $250-285. Brown felt envelope handbag, satin lined, brass engraved triangle on flap, $85-95. Brown brimmed felt cloche hat, $30-35. (WWII) military uniform, jacket with decorations, $85-95. Complete uniform, $100-110.

1942. Short crepe 'dressy' dresses, flattering and slimming. $125-135. Courtesy Butterick Archives.

Cocktail dress, 1945. Black crepe top, V-off the shoulder neck, ruffled tiers of black net over taffeta skirt. Net and embroidered see-through shoes. Value, dress, $120-150; shoes, $45-65.

Black crepe mid-calf length dress, V-neck, belted. C. 1949, black satin shoes with self bows, original to the costume. Double strand pearl choker, pink. Values: dress, $125-135; shoes, $60-80.

Gray wool two piece suit, lined. Pearl buttons, Eisenhower jacket, c. 1945. Value, $100-125.

1950. Light pink strapless taffeta evening gown with large bow accenting one shoulder. Full skirt lined with a stiffened attached slip. Value, $100-125.

C. 1949-1950 'formal'. Black silk velvet top, with striped black and white skirt. A spectacular dress. Value, $125-145.

1951, 2 piece red velvet afternoon outfit. Rhinestone buttons, short fitted jacket, lace over velvet collar. Red felt hat and dark red shoes, all original to the dress. Dress, 2 pieces, value, $95-125. Hat, with black beading, $25-30. Shoes, $30-35.

1964 Mini skirt dress in cotton, value, $45-55. Photo courtesy of Butterick Archives.

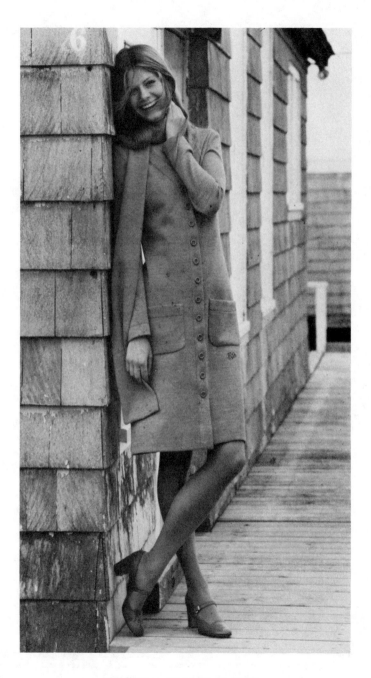

1968 Knitwear full length coat, $50-55.

The still popular silver fox jacket, c. 1941. Value, $650-750. Black satin evening dress, c. 1935. Value $195-220. Satin shoes, worn originally with the dress shown, buckles are part of shoe itself, $75-100.

Full length wool coat with classic white fox collar; brown with bands of contrasting darker brown.
C. 1950. Value, $750-850.

Sweaters of the 1950's. Black one beaded, white is 2 piece set, sequined over all, both hand beaded and sequined, all are silk lined. Beaded fringe on the white undersweater. These were usually made in Japan or Hong Kong of lambswool or cashmere, and the better examples such as these could never be produced again with such fine hand work at any reasonable price. Black, value, $65-85. White set, value $100-135.

1949. Spring hats in straw. Hats of this type range $30-35, but they must be in perfect condition.

Accessories: alligator shoes, sharply pointed toe, 1957. Value $75-100. Corde handbag, plastic handle, 1942. Value, $30-35. Alligator handbag, 1952. Value $100-135.

Hawaiian shirts, these early shirts are highly collectible, left to right: cotton print, coconut buttons; center, photograph silk-screened onto rayon; Hawaiian tropical flowers, background is picture of philodendrum superimposed. Called double prints. C. 1940's, early 1950's. Shirts of this type were originally worn by entertainers. Values, $35-65.

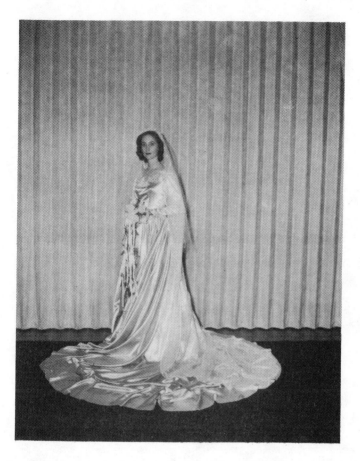

Formal wedding gown, 1951. Candlelight satin, appliqued leaves and seed pearls at neck. Train. Value, $750-850.